God Knows Your Measure

A Journey to Rediscovering Your Faith

Venesia,
God has
Confidence
in ♡You!

[signature]

Crystal M. Roberts

Crystal M. Roberts
Jacksonville, NC, US 28546
www.CrystalMRoberts.com

Ordering Information:
For details, contact thecrystalmroberts@gmail.com.

Print ISBN: 978-0-578-86158-6

Scriptures quoted are taken from the KING JAMES VERSION (KJV): KING JAMES VERSION, public domain.

Printed in the United States of America on SFI Certified paper.

First Edition

Dedication

This book is dedicated to my amazing mother, Patricia Ann (Lloyd) Tate-Graham, who transitioned on May 13, 2020. She was the perfect example of God's love, humility, forgiveness, patience, and gentleness. She raised eleven intelligent, talented, and wonderful children, encouraging and supporting us in everything we put our hands to. She loved and served people the way God instructed her to until she took her last breath. I was blessed to be able to share *God Knows Your Measure* with her before I moved to North Carolina in 2017, after which she lovingly admonished me, "...do not forget your book."
Mommy, I love you forever and always.

I present to the world my first book, *God Knows Your Measure*. I pray you are encouraged, enlightened, and strengthened.
Be Blessed.

Table of Contents

Foreword

I met Crystal Roberts some years ago at my church, Free and Independent Apostolic Church, Inc. When she came to visit, the Lord spoke a word through me, to her, about relocating. She did not think twice to make the move because it was the will of God. I have watched this young lady go through transformations both naturally, mentally, and spiritually, and I have seen her get the victory she deserved.

She has chosen Job as her test character for her book, and what a character to use. Going through unprecedented trials and tribulations, seeming to be at the will of God and the way of God, he endured the ultimate test of the Father to prove Him right and the enemy wrong. I believe everyone goes through their own personal Job experience; he lost it all, and everyone has an idea of what *all* is to them.

This book, God Knows Your Measure by Crystal Roberts, expresses the chronicles of her life: her mistakes, her triumphs, her tests, and how she came through it all. While the Bible is an amazing book, a person's life experience that you can see, talk to, and get advice from can hit a little harder because the author is with us and not in a book. Read this book, take the lessons learned from the book and use it to help guide your life. I am absolutely proud of Crystal Roberts. I pray this book reaches the nations for the cause of Christ and holistic healing. Blessings to all who shall buy and read this book in Jesus' name!

Foreword written in love and respect by
Dr. Keith K. Curry

Introduction

The story of Job is about a blessed man whom God offered up into Satan's hands to prove that he wouldn't curse Him. We learn that this perfect man was stripped of everything he had: his children, his substance, and lastly, his health. While his wife turned against him, some friends came to comfort him. Throughout Job's suffering, the highlighted and magnified statements etched in our minds are, "though He slay me, yet will I trust in Him" and "all my appointed time, I'm going to wait until my change come." However, we like to skip through Job's story to the "good" parts. We start with how he was a blessed man who lost everything by the hand of Satan because of God's confidence in him. Then we skip to the middle of the story where Job's hope is reassured and he says, "though He slay me . . ." and "all the days of my appointed time will I wait." Lastly, we jump to the very end where Job receives "double for his trouble"—and we are all encouraged.

While these are all key points of his life, and his hope is reassured in these scriptures, there is a lot Job says in between that proves he wasn't flawless. It allows us to see that he was human, just like us. Though he feared God and lived a life admired by all, Job had some issues that needed to be squeezed out of him. Job knew God, but only to an extent. Throughout his suffering, Job spoke very foolishly and, to my surprise, it wasn't accounted to him as a curse to God. As you read through this book, *God Knows Your Measure*, examining the entire story of Job, you will see sides of Job that we don't often hear about. Job didn't always have it all together. He meant well, but the suffering God allowed was very necessary to purge all the things that weren't quite like Him, and to prove Job's life before Him.

Even though Job spoke without complete knowledge and

wisdom, God still had grace and mercy on him. God knew Job was flawed. God said Job wouldn't curse Him, and He never flinched concerning that. Because God said it, He brought Job through it all.

The book of Job has always been a story I desired to read, and truly understand, because of what I have observed over the years, mainly in the church. The majority seem to be so closed-mouthed when suffering. In our silence, being so closed off, we misunderstand strength. We try so hard to make suffering look good and effortless when, in reality, we are hurting beyond expression. We avoid talking to anyone about the truth of our suffering. We may express everything, but avoid the realness of what we've experienced or are experiencing, saying, "Oh, yes I've been through that, but with God I made it out." In this "testimony" we are missing the depths of what one has gone through: the crevasses and dark places that we didn't believe we'd climb out of. We don't express our depression; we don't express how deeply broken we were. We lead people to believe that the pain isn't so bad. Even if it is that bad, and one begins to express themselves by showing deeply felt emotions and frustrations, some people act as if it's foreign to simply *feel*. Some believers can make it seem a sign of weakness that we feel what is sure: the heaviness of our afflictions. In this process, we miss that there is strength in our vulnerability—strength that can go from heart to heart.

For so long, when I felt down in the dumps about my situations, I believed that I was supposed to just put a smile on my face—and I did, while quoting scriptures. I believed that if I spoke out honestly about my pain and confusion, if I were to show that I was angry or that things were too heavy for me, it meant that I was *fainting*. The Bible says, "We shall reap if we faint not" *(Galatians 6:9)*. How could I reap if I was feeling down or frustrated about what I had to go through? In those times, I was truly discouraged. For years, I didn't understand what fainting was. I didn't understand what the depth of unwavering faith was. I didn't understand how I could be human and also stand confident before God. Now, having walked through a few personal crises, I truly understand that the love of God is unexplainable. I was giving up on God at one point. I was in so much pain and confusion! I just didn't want to care anymore. As I expressed those things to God, He encouraged me. When I began to be very real before God, fully pouring out my heart before Him, He comforted me. Had He not given me the measure of love, grace, and forgiveness I needed to get through those moments in my life, I would not be here to tell my story.

God has given each of us the necessary measure that we need to stand with Him and before Him. God will not allow anything to come our way that will destroy us. If we delight in the Lord and trust in Him with all our hearts, He will no doubt protect us and keep us.

This book, *God Knows Your Measure*, is about the grace and mercy given to Job in the heart of his affliction and unimaginable pain. One thing that I desire for you to take away from *God Knows Your Measure* is that it's okay to feel! It's okay to be frustrated and confused. It's okay to feel weak and indescribably pained. It's okay—simply because God has created us this way. We don't always understand what God is doing, yet if we remember that He is God, we will be strengthened by His might. So whatever emotion God has blessed you to experience, experience it unapologetically! Feel what He has allowed, but don't allow the emotions to consume you in such a way that you turn your heart from God, forgetting who He is. Experiencing your emotions is valid; let it turn your heart towards God that He may restore and encourage you. God knows what you can handle and He equips you with the measure necessary to survive and experience great victory.

God knows your measure.

CHAPTER 1

Job:
From Peace to Despair
(Job 1-3)

Job's Life Before the Affliction

Job was a righteous man. He was married to one wife and had ten children: seven sons and three daughters. Besides that, he was blessed with much substance. Job not only made certain that he was covered by the sacrifices he offered to God, but also made sure that he covered his children. He overcompensated to keep his name clear, careful not to offend God in any way. Job honored God with his entire house. He wanted God to attest to how much he honored and loved Him. He needed his pathway and worship before God to be clear. Job did not want there to be any reason for God to be displeased or disappointed with him.

God and Satan

One day, as the sons of God were gathering together to stand before Him, Satan came also. God noticed him, of course, and asked him where he was coming from. Satan responded that he was simply walking about the earth. Satan had seen all the people coming together to worship God; what better place to stop by? Satan's only agenda was, and is, to find the precious jewels of God's Kingdom and dismantle them. Job was a precious jewel, and Satan knew that. But because of God's hedge of protection around Job, he recognized he could never turn Job's heart from Him.

God decided to challenge Satan—He offered Job to him, declaring Job's faithfulness (Job 1:8). So, God took away the hedge of protection from all of Job's wealth and family. God then gave Satan permission to touch all Job had, but his body was off limits. He told Satan to do as he pleased within the lines of those specific instructions. In an instant, Satan left God's presence to carry out his mission.

"Behold, all that he hath is in thy power; only upon himself put not forth thine hand . . ."
Job 1:12a

Something that stands out to me: Satan needed permission to try

3

Job. I truly believe, by Satan's reply to God, that he had considered Job before. He just never pursued Job because he was well protected. Satan assumed the only reason Job feared and lived an honorable life before God was because he was abundantly blessed. Therefore Satan knew tampering with Job and all he had was a losing battle, and he'd never bothered him.

Had God not given Satan permission and free range, Job would not have had to endure such turmoil. He was said to be the greatest man in the east. Satan knew that Job was perfect, everyone knew— but Satan didn't know the depths of Job's heart. Even though Job had a perfect life and had everything one could hope for, he did not let what he had obtained get into his heart and compromise his integrity and love for God. Job knew it was only by the hand of God that he had gained so much. I learned that, not only was Satan unclear of the depths of Job's heart, Job himself was unaware. But God knew, without a shadow of a doubt, that he was totally committed to Him. Nevertheless, it would all soon unfold and become plain to all.

Was Job Religious?

While Job was very devoted to God, honoring Him with his entire house and going the extra mile to cover his children's possible sins, the latter part of Chapter 1 shows that he was neither practicing vain repetitions nor just following the ways of the holy land and his forefathers. Job was as invested as one could be for God, for he knew the ways of God. Although Job needed a greater understanding of his relationship with God, and who God was, his foundation was sure. He seemed to be justified by his works, but Job's service to God was pure. He truly feared God; he reverenced Him.

God gave Satan authority to attack all Job had. Satan took his wealth and his children, sparing only one servant per field, and one person who witnessed the death of his children and could give the heart-wrenching news to Job. Back to back, four different servants came to Job to share with him the news that Satan hoped would break him.

In Job 1:20–22, it showed that Job was not just a religious man, but he was truly committed to God. Job was very grieved. He shaved his head, tore his mantle, and lost all strength in his time of pain. Although he was experiencing great sorrow, Job worshipped God after receiving such horrible news. Job still gave glory and praise to God in that devastating place.

Job praised God in this impossible situation that most would crumble under. In an instant, Job experienced the great loss of his ten children. Even before he received the news about his children, he'd heard of the loss of his land and animals; in a moment it was all gone. Amazingly, in the loss of everything, Job never forgot that all his possessions came from God. Had Job not realized that all he had had come from God, he would have had a different disposition. He would have had a different response. Job said, "the Lord gave, and the Lord hath taketh away" *(Job 1:21b)*. At that point, he knew and allowed all to see where his heart rested. Job was confident that he would be alright

"Naked came I out of my mother's womb, and naked shall I return thither: the Lord gave, and He hath taken away; blessed be the name of the Lord."
Job 1:21

because he served the Almighty God. Job's response is the ultimate praise and reverence because it wasn't at Job's reception where his praise and reverence for God stood—it was at everything being stripped from him. The Word of God then declares that Job didn't sin nor speak foolishly of God or toward what He had allowed *(Job 1:22)*.

God and Satan
Once again, Satan was roaming about and made his presence

known before God, as the sons of God gathered before Him. <u>It is safe to say that a group or body of believers gathering together alerts Satan and draws him near to see what's going on.</u> Again, God acknowledged Satan, who replied that he was still walking throughout the earth, east to west; he was on his own personal assignment. God then offered up Job to Satan for a second time, still boasting about his devout servant! God expressed to Satan that his plans and thoughts of Job crumbling had been false, and that Job stood strong even in his pain. God told Satan: in the whole earth, no one measured up to Job. How amazing! God spoke highly of Job, and made very clear Job's credentials before Satan, knowing that Job would not curse Him. Although Satan provoked God to test Job for no reason at all, God knew Job and had confidence in him.

Again, Satan made a false accusation: that if Job's body were afflicted, he would curse God. Satan was desperate and believed that he had the power and ability to turn Job's heart against God. He wanted to prove to God that he had the ability to turn a very precious and upright man against Him with any type of tactic or scheme. But Satan was wrong. After his first failed attempt, perhaps his pride wouldn't let him give up. His desire was to make God out to be a liar. So Satan made more and more excuses as to why Job's heart was actually set on Him. Poor Satan!

". . . that there is none like him in the earth, a perfect and upright man, one that escheweth evil? And still holdest fast his integrity, to destroy him without cause."
Job 2:3

So God instructed Satan to touch Job's body, but he was not allowed to kill him.

Job and Satan

Then Satan, without hesitation, afflicted Job's entire body with

6

sore boils, which Job had to scrape with a potsherd. A potsherd is a piece of ceramic material, a broken fragment of pottery. When Job's body was afflicted, he initially did not say a word. As he sat grieving in ashes, he silently and immediately did what he had to do to take care of his skin's condition. He was distraught, but still holding on.

Without his usual hedge of protection, Job did not curse God, as Satan claimed!

On the other hand, Job's wife, who had been silent up until this point, was hurt and in utter disbelief at what this "great God" had allowed to happen to such a perfect man, wholly devoted to God. She, too, had experienced the great loss of all her children and was directly affected by the loss of their wealth. Now she was seeing her husband, who had done no wrong toward God and who feared Him, suffer such affliction and pain. She was offended! She was broken! She was pressed up against a wall because the life she had known had been completely flipped—upside down and inside out. So, because of her brokenness and lack of relationship and understanding with God for herself, she told her husband (who feared God) to just give up. "Curse God, and die"(Job 2:9).

Job's wife tried to encourage him to stop fighting and standing for God. She saw no point in continuing to do so. God, in her eyes, had wrongfully dealt with her husband, who had only loved Him. She didn't want to see Job suffer any longer, for her sake or his own. Job's response to his wife was more proof that he was not one to rehearse the repetitions of those who claimed to "serve" God. He proved he was a true servant of God, one who recognized the might of God. Job told his wife that she spoke as an ignorant woman, one who did not know the true essence of God. As Job was trying to understand all of what was happening, he simultaneously tried to open his wife's eyes to the mere fact and infallible truth

"Doth thou still retain thine integrity? Curse God, and die." Job 2:9

7

that God is just! Job expressed to her the greatness of God by stating one question: "What? Shall we only receive good at the hand of God, and shall we not receive evil?"(Job 2:10b).

Job, once again, didn't speak against God, even though he didn't understand the reasons behind his sufferings. Though his children had been taken away, with all his wealth and substance, and now his health attacked and wife giving up, he still held onto God's sovereignty. He still reverenced the Creator of heaven and earth. Amid his turmoil and unfamiliar place, his foundation was sure and built on the fear he had for the Almighty God.

Job and Friends

After all these great and terrible things, Job's friends, Eliphaz, Bildad, and Zophar, came to visit him. They knew Job as a devout servant of God. They knew him as an upright man who was wealthy and prosperous. Bad news travels fast, and when you are in the spotlight and known for being great, it is bound to spread more rapidly. Job's friends were not from the same city as him nor did they live in the same cities as each other. They traveled from three different areas to gather and be of support to Job as best they could.

When Job's friends made it to his home, they could not recognize him from afar. He was so distraught, beat down, and weak—the total opposite of his reputation and stature—that his friends felt his pain and began to cry with loud voices. They even tore their clothes and sprinkled ashes on their heads, as Job did, as a sign of despair. Because Job was deeply grieved and miserable, his friends sat down on the ground with him, in silence, for seven days and seven nights.

After the seven days and nights of silence, Job spoke. When he opened his mouth, without hesitation, he cursed the day he was born. He was heartbroken, experiencing pain unlike any other time in his

8

life. He wished for darkness to consume that day, and desired for his birth to be forgotten and removed from time.

In Job's expression, he asked many questions surrounding the purpose for which he survived the womb. What was the reason he survived—just to live a life of such misery? Why was life given to those in distress? Job was hurt and he expressed it vividly. He was confused and extremely uncomfortable!

Job was completely flawless in the sight of man. He was admired by all. He was known for the life he lived unto God. He was a good person, and he was undoubtedly blessed. When we live a life such as this, God continuously looks past our faults and imperfections, and sees the very intent of our hearts. He is God! He knows every single issue embedded in our very make up. He created us. Job loved and feared God, but he had problems beyond the surface. Even though he walked in righteousness, shunning evil and honoring God with everything he had, he wasn't without fault. He was a prosperous man, in health and wealth. He appreciated who God was to him and praised God for how He had fashioned him.

Despite being well known as this perfect and upright man who feared God, and being the greatest man in the east, all he wanted to do in this place of torment was die. In this moment, his reputation didn't matter to him. He was losing his fight. Most would say he was failing his test. But in actuality, **Job was just human**. Job showed a side of himself that we often hide, as believers. Job was feeling pain and anguish, and he expressed it. As he articulated so clearly his thoughts and emotions, I would say he tried to be careful not to say anything directly cursing God. He expressed his misery and confusion to his friends in this moment, and we will read later on how He also expressed it to God.

One thing I have learned through Job's story is that it's okay to feel! The Bible says, "Be ye angry, and sin not" (Ephesians 4:26). This gives us a clear understanding that we can freely be angry—it is simply an emotion that will be felt in this flesh. We are human! It is okay to express such emotion, but in that place we should still exhibit self-control. That is what keeps us from stepping over that forbidden fence. The depths of Job's emotions in this place were expressed as such; he would rejoice if he could have found his grave because the only thing he now longed for was death. The weight had become very heavy, awfully fast! The scriptures explain: the exact thing Job feared, he was now dwelling in. Though he was calling out to God, he found no rest, safety, or comfort. Trouble seemed to constantly consume him. (Job 3:20–26)

But even in this place, Satan was still wrong; Job did not curse God!

CHAPTER 2

Eliphaz:
Job's Innocence Challenged
(Job 4-7)

Job was an example to all who knew him. I imagine he was sort of idolized as to what a relationship with God looked like. He was probably who his friends and neighbors patterned their lives after. So after this great "fall," as some people viewed it, they began to question Job and his relationship with God. Rightfully so, being that they looked toward him as the man he was: faultless, respectable, one who honored God and disclaimed evil. How could such wickedness come into the house of such a devoted and honest man? So his friends set out to reason with him—not only for Job's sake, to try to help him understand why, in their individual perspectives, he was in this darkness, but also for their own understanding and clarification.

Their view of righteousness seemed to be based on Job's perfection and all they were taught by their fathers and elders, so now their view was a bit distorted. Job's friends were certain of whom they knew God to be; Job had to have done something to receive such trouble and chastisement. From the past days of the law, as written in Deuteronomy 28, you are blessed if you follow and obey the commands of God and cursed if you don't. With that understanding, the people had every right to want to figure out what exactly was going on. They were also confused.

Eliphaz and Job

Job's friend Eliphaz expressed to him that he could not possibly be innocent, suffering so much pain. Job had been an encouragement to so many people. He was one to strengthen those who were weak and help those in need. Eliphaz then pointed out how the tables had turned: now Job was the one weak and in need, yet he could not find any refuge.

How was it that Job could pour into so many, yet fall at those very troubles? Eliphaz questioned Job: being one who fears and honors God, and knowing Him and all His ways—where was his confidence in the God he served, and had been serving all this time?

> *"But now it is come upon thee, and thou faintest; it toucheth thee and thou art troubled."*
> *Job 4:5*

Eliphaz proceeded to express to Job, who was already devastated, that he must have done something wrong. Eliphaz implied that the innocent do not suffer. God did not punish the upright and those who fear Him! Eliphaz wanted to know from Job's mouth: what did he do?

Job, What Did You Do?

Eliphaz was sold on the idea that Job had sinned or brought this hardship and depression on himself, not knowing God orchestrated the whole thing. God was still with Job, but his friend was not aware of this, nor was Job.

> *"Even as I have seen, they that plow iniquity, and sow wickedness, reap the same."*
> *Job 4:8*

Eliphaz had a vision in which it was spoken, "Shall mortal man be more just than God? Shall a man be more pure than his Maker?" (Job 4:17). If God did not trust His servants, who were heavenly, and if His angels were pure, how much trust could God possibly have in those who dwelled in this sinful flesh? All of this to say: could any man be as perfect as God? Was not God the only perfect and innocent being?

Eliphaz went on speaking to Job about how faithful God was and had been. He told him: trouble did not just come out of thin air or appear out of the ground. Man is born into trouble. We cannot escape it. Trouble is as sure as the sparks that fly (Job 5:7).

Eliphaz expressed that Job would have been better off just admitting to God his wrongs and pleading his case to Him. Because God was merciful and marvelous, He would forgive Job and fix this whole situation. He would bring Job out of his misery into a place of safety and liberty: He's God. He was the God who helped us in our *time of trouble. God would deliver Job, if he would only ask Him; if he would just confess. Eliphaz urged Job to lean towards God to make things right. It's understood that the chastisement of the Lord was good, and Job needed to count his suffering as a blessing and honor.*

All the land saw Job as a perfect man, and no doubt believed and claimed the same. Job was faultless in the sight of people, yet he was flawed, in a sense, with a heart to worship God. He didn't entertain evil in deed or in thought; Job wasn't malicious, immoral, or an intentional sinner, but he was made to suffer to prove to Satan that God's word was sure.

One question I asked myself, as stated in the previous chapter: Does Job harbor pride? Being that he was "the man"—this great example—and that there was none like him on the whole earth, could pride have settled in?

One thing I've learned is that trials come to clean us out. Suffering allows us to experience who and where we truly are. It reveals to us our strength and whether we are learning and growing towards the image and likeness we were created in. This time of suffering and affliction for Job revealed a lot that was bottled up in him. It revealed things that would have never been exposed had God not allowed Satan to afflict him. God had to prove to Satan, for Satan's awareness, that all that was said and seen of Job was solid.

While all of this was true on God's behalf, Eliphaz was accusing Job of being in sin and not confessing it. He was trying to help Job to understand the faithfulness of God, and that God protected the righteous. God could grant Job peace again, if he would just understand and apply everything Eliphaz had pointed out to him.

Job's Defense

After giving ear to what Eliphaz had said, Job communicated how disappointed he was with him. Job was upset by the accusations put against him. All he wanted from his friends was comfort and compassion. He had already lost everything and was now battling with his health, but Eliphaz came to him with words of shame, adding more sorrow.

Job already did not quite understand what he was facing, but he knew God was above all and could do whatever He pleased. However, Job believed that God had forsaken him. Job was extremely heavy. He just wanted to die. He saw no point or hope in living another second. He longed for God to loosen His hand from him and just end his life.

As Job listened to his friend, he compared him to being as useless as a frozen stream—as useless as a body of water once enlarged, but now small and dried up. He found his friends as disappointing as a useless dried up stream people had once used to get from one place to the other. What the travelers expected to see was now gone. It was nothing but a wasteland—a barren land—and that was how Job now viewed his friends: useless.

Job was hurt by his friends. He posed questions to them, asking: did he ask for them to come see him? Did he ask them for any money to help him replenish all he had lost, or for them to save him from his nightmare? Job did not reach out to them for help; they had willingly come. He begged them to tell him what he did wrong—he would hear everything they had to say. But until they could prove that he had done wrong, Job refused to give ear to them.

Job's friends lacked compassion in the way he needed it. Considering all he was suffering, Job felt like he deserved at least that—compassion. Job did not want his reputation or his name to be forgotten, so he reminded his friends who he was. He urged his friends to really look at him and remember who they had known him to be. Then, he told them to judge him accordingly and not based on what they guessed was true. Job was determined to prove that he was an honorable man and did not deserve all he was facing (Job 6:27).

All in all, Job was living in a nightmare and he desired to be free of the constant pain and agony! He was restless and becoming very hopeless, wondering when or even if his morning would come. His body was covered with worms and his skin was disgusting. He was now living in complete torment, well beyond what he believed he was worthy of.

"My flesh is clothed with worms and clods of dust; my skin is broken, and become loathsome."
Job 7:5

Many times, we are all in that place, trying our best to live a "perfect" life. Then, when we suffer with things such as illnesses or financial burdens, we feel we are too "worthy" to experience such. We have a self-righteous belief that we have somehow earned God's grace and mercy. We believe that we have somehow deserved God's pouring down of endless blessings. *News Flash Family:* we haven't earned anything. We don't *deserve* anything. So, I recognized that Job had some pride in his members, as early as his first response to his friends.

"So that my soul chooseth strangling, and death rather than my life."
Job 7:15

What Is Cursing God?

Job was in unimaginable pain and discomfort. He was in anguish! He spoke out very strongly and declared that as long as he was in pain, he would continue to speak out and make his voice heard. He refused to keep silent. He was choosing to not hold back the authentic expression of his pain. Job was a human being: wrapped in flesh. We must remember that. We can't be afraid or too reserved in

17

sharing how we feel with our friends or confidants, our brothers and sisters in Christ. Keeping silent in this place is more detrimental. As long as the intensity of our emotions doesn't cause us to sin by our words and actions and curse God, we can feel what we feel and talk about it. Even then, God has given each of us a certain measure of grace and mercy that will carry us through our appointed times of affliction.

I believe *cursing God* is challenging His authority with the fruit of our lips, influenced by the depths of our heart. I believe it's doubting the pure essence and might of God and turning away from Him, denouncing that He is God—especially after walking with God, experiencing the goods, and partaking of the Holy Ghost *(Hebrews 6:4–6)*.

Crossing that line, cursing God, is not at all tolerated by God. It allows the enemy to win, proving that we were never really *for* God. It would prove God to be a liar. If God is presenting us before Satan, bragging on our footing in Him, we must know that we can stand **any** test! God is not a liar and can never be made out to be. With God in us and with us, the enemy will always come out a loser. We are champions through Christ Jesus, through the Spirit of God!

Job and God

Job was ready to give up the fight. He began to hate his life—he did not see any more value in it—and just wanted to be left alone. This once perfect and honorable man who feared God now felt that his new price tag was worse than dust. He wondered why God even thought of man, creating and forming them out of mere clay. Job was full of unanswered questions. He wondered: if he was formed from the dust of the earth, from nothing, why did God see fit to hold on to him? He wondered: why would God allow him to wake up, if suffering was all he was made to endure? Job constantly wondered and asked these things.

18

Ultimately, the question Job wanted answered was, why did he have to suffer? Job asked God: what should he do to make things right, if he had sinned against Him? Why would God keep him around if he was no use to anyone and was the only one who had to bear such horrible consequences? Why was God neglecting to save him from this great punishment? What did he do wrong? If Job had done something wrong, why was not God revealing it to him? Job was terribly confused and in massive pain, and he just wanted it all to be over. He wanted to go to sleep and remain there.

"I have sinned; what shall I do unto Thee, O Thou preserver of men? Why has Thou set me a mark against thee, so that I am a burden to myself?"
Job 7:20

Even so, Satan was still wrong about Job. Job did not curse God!

In this place, it's hard to understand or accept that God was with Job. Even as Job outwardly expressed to God and his friends the raw emotions of his current situation, he never stepped over that boundary. God was still being glorified above Satan. We must remember that God is always in our corner. We can say how we feel in the rawest and realest way before God, because He understands. He is our God, and He is our Father. He is not so far away that we cannot reach Him. God will always be right there beside us to console and help us. We just need to understand that all we need is in His bosom!

God wants us to be completely open and vulnerable with Him. He wants that open line of communication between Himself and each of us. He wants to know what is on our minds, how we really feel. He wants us to cry out before Him and release every single concern or matter. He wants us to be comfortable with Him. It is in those moments that we're able to release and empty out what weighs us

19

down.

God is the only One who can handle our weight. He is the only One who can fix our problems. He is the only One who will always be with us, until the end of the world, because He will forever be.

Be open and express yourself to God. Feel free to feel, you are human; God created us that way! Learn to pour out your heart before God so that you can exhale smoothly and live without the stress and weariness of issues only He understands. God absolutely has your back. Even though sometimes we may not hear Him or feel Him, we must know that He is omnipresent. God is everywhere, He hears and sees everything. Silence from Him is how He knows whether He is truly in our hearts or not. God is vouching for us and knows what our end is. If He said we can win, we can! If He tells the devil to consider us, know that we will trample over all the enemy places in our path. We must trust God.

"Casting all your care upon Him; for He careth for you."
1 Peter 5:7

In Job 4–5, Job's innocence was challenged by his dear friend Eliphaz. Though Job articulated and demonstrated many human emotions, he continually fought for his faith. It was all he had left. Although he felt God forsook him, Job never stopped trusting in Him, hence his fight. When you don't give up the fight, when you choose to go before God to figure out what's going on, it is evident that you are holding on strong to what you believe. You know that your hope rests in God. That's the perfect attitude to possess! Never give up, and keep trusting God!

CHAPTER 3

Bildad & Zophar:
God Is Not a Liar
(Job 8-14)

Bildad and Job

Once again, Job's friends laid grief on him. Bildad, Job's second friend, wanted to know how long Job would defend himself so strongly. Given that God was sure and certainly amazing, Bildad did not understand how Job could be so combative and so confident of himself. Job clearly wasn't backing down, because he knew he had not made a mistake that caused his great affliction. On the other hand, his friends could not accept that God would lie. Bildad knew the history of his land, his forefathers, how they walked, and what they taught. In so many words, he inquired: would God really cause the innocent and upright to lack in any way; would He cause them to die? Would God cause them to suffer?

Bildad agreed strongly with Eliphaz, because they knew that God would only bless His children and torment the evil doers. It was how things were. It was how they knew God operated. Bildad urged Job to look back and remember the old and faithful ways of God. They recognized God as the One to reward those obedient to His voice and commands. They understood, following the blueprint of what salvation was known to be at that time, that there was no distress involved. How could the obedient suffer? There was absolutely no way, if you stayed on course and honored God, a curse would be granted to you.

Was Job now shining a different light on the true essence of a relationship with God? Being that he didn't do any wrong yet was now experiencing a great deal of suffering, what was this now teaching him and all those who followed him?

Job responded to his friend, agreeing with everything he mentioned. Job had never ignored the fact that God blessed the righteous; he was aware of it. He was blessed beyond measure! Job was the one people gravitated to and reached out to when they had

23

trouble. As mentioned several times, Job was ". . . the greatest of all the men in the east" (Job 1:3). Job then said to his friends: how could man be perfect and without fault before God? How could we be in a place where we know just as much as God, or stand on the same pedestal as our God?

Job knew, in his logic and all he had learned, that he could never be God or be compared to Him. He also knew that he could never contend against God. Yet he did so repeatedly as he spoke through his pain and confusion. Job tried his best to remain humble before God, but this was a pain he had never experienced before. He spoke everything he knew of the law of the land and the law of the Lord, but he also spoke out of his mouth very foolish things that coincided with his limited understanding of God's judgment.

Job understood that no matter if he was guilty or innocent, God was still God. Job knew he was unworthy to challenge Him. And that God, without reason, could destroy anyone or anything simply because He's God. Job wanted to make sure his friends comprehended he wasn't oblivious to the mighty hand of God, regardless of what things looked like.

Job declared that even though he was truly without blame, he still hated his life. Even if he could prove his innocence, it meant nothing because God held total power to destroy all men, good or bad.

**"This is one thing, therefore I said it, He destroyeth the perfect and the wicked."
Job 9:22**

Job continued, "If I say, I will forget my complaint, I will leave off my heaviness, and comfort myself: I am afraid of all my sorrows, I know that Thou will not hold me innocent" (Job 9:27–28). Placing a smile on his face, turning his frown upside down as if everything were fine—Job could have done that. He could have stopped complaining about his pain and forgotten it all for a moment. However, he would still be terrified because God would not attest to his innocence. As Job understood, not only were his friends against him, so was God. Job would much rather be honest in his moments of affliction, and express his truth. He would rather rest in the darkness of his suffering because it was what he had to bear; God caused it to come into his life.

Job was burdened by and afraid of all that had befallen him, but the fact that his character was now challenged weighed even heavier. He was not known or recognized as a righteous man any longer, and that was difficult for him. So he continued to defend himself. He said why would he have done so much good, if his intentions were always evil? (Job 9:29). Job desperately desired for someone to help him understand God's reasoning for appointing such a dreadful place, and save him. Then, he wouldn't be so afraid; he would speak in peace about everything. If he could understand, he could have hope!

Job's Death: More Desirable than His Pain

Job obnoxiously refused to keep quiet about his pain. It was bad! The more his friends "comforted" him, the worse he felt. Job often asked God to leave him alone. He expressed to God: He was the One who created him, fashioned and molded him. So, only He knew if he had sinned. Job pleaded with God to enlighten him on where he failed, where he stumbled. He wanted God to mend this broken place and cause peace during his storm. He desired for God to hear his cry and take the pain away. Job wanted answers! He understood that God wasn't obligated to explain His purpose for the suffering He allowed, but Job was desperate to know what was going on. So he asked over and over again.

Job repeatedly asked God: why did He allow him to be born into this world instead of sending him straight to the grave? Since he was enduring such unexplained suffering, why not just kill him at the very moment of conception?

Again, Job would have preferred to escape life. He wanted God to depart from him so he wouldn't feel any more pain. He felt he would eventually only disappoint God and fall into a pit of no return. Job was scared that he wouldn't make it out of such a dark, confusing, and loathsome place. His heart eagerly wanted to please God, but he did not know if he was strong enough to hold on.

There was a time in my life when I, too, wished I was aborted or miscarried, never to have seen the light of day. A time when I felt no one cared about me or loved me. At that time, I needed so much from those around me, especially those who were "supposed" to love and nourish me. I felt abandoned and neglected by my parents, who, in my opinion, were required to love and accept me. I didn't understand the point of birthing me if I would still fail to matter, or be a mere factor in their lives—or anyone else's, for that matter. At that time, I never felt preferred or noticed by my family, nor by those I wanted to simply like me. So my thoughts were, "Why should I have to be in this world? I didn't ask to be here."

When I was in a relationship that was "perfect," yet against the will of God, there were times when death seemed easier to bear than the pain of having to let this man go. It was hard, even impossible, for me. The fact that I had searched and waited for a "love" like the one that found me was amazing. Yet this "love" wasn't love—not what I needed or waited for. I later learned it wasn't anything more than lust, and it was tortuous because of its great limits: he couldn't commit to me. Seeing him outside of our encounters was excruciating and heart wrenching. I never intended to have to bear such agony in my life. While Job's afflictions weren't caused by his sins, as were mine, he too saw death as an easier and less painful way out. I never in my life thought that I would be in such a relationship that felt so right, yet be so wrong by the laws of the land and, most importantly, by the laws of God. I never wanted or desired such, but it is what I experienced. Great unexplainable distress and misery accompanied it. My affliction, just like Job's, though, mirrored and brought to the surface impurities in my heart. It was also a tool, purifying me to tell my story and testimony of how God's love can pull someone through darkness, through seemingly impossible situations.

Zophar and Job

Job's third friend stepped forward and his viewpoint. He, like the other two friends, called Job a liar, in so many words. As Job continued to defend his innocence, standing firm on his track record before God, Zophar wondered if Job really thought they should believe him. Nevertheless, Job desperately wanted God to just reveal to him the reasons for all the misery and loss he was enduring.

Zophar, his friend, also pointed out that Job should be grateful God was not giving him the entirety of what he deserved. All of Job's friends were expressing how great and just God was. And none of what Job explained to them was making any kind of sense.

Job's Wisdom Challenged

Job's story was not lining up with who they had grown to know God to be and how He operated. They were extremely knowledgeable of God's fairness that would not reward sins with blessings. He would not allow those who did evil to receive prosperity. They knew God was not a liar, so Job had to be—bottom line. Regardless of what they knew about Job's unquestionable character prior to this moment in his life, they held onto who they served. They held onto God, who was above all, who was great in wisdom, and whose existence was perfection. God was higher than any other; no one came before Him, and no one was worthy enough to come after Him. God could not make a mistake, but Job was well able. They were defending and standing up for their God! Perhaps, the foundation of their faith would have been shaken if they had believed Job was without fault and did nothing to cause his affliction. What kind of God were they really serving? One who would cause or allow affliction for no valid reason? They could not believe that for one second.

Zophar, too, advised Job to confess his sins so God would allow him to be free. He advised him to stop resting in wickedness—then all would be well. Job would no longer experience the fear, horrible dreams, or sleepless nights. Then, Job's morning, his restoration, would be certain. If he would just come clean, God would forgive him and show him mercy, Zophar exclaimed.

"But I have understanding as well as you; I am not inferior to you: yea, who knoweth not such things as these?"
Job 12:3

Job responded to Zophar, as well as the other two friends, and challenged their wisdom. Job attested to their wisdom, yet in the same breath he expressed that he, too, knew and understood all the things they did not hesitate to confront him with. Their conversation did not intimidate Job.

Once more, Job explained his relationship with God to his friends. He knew God and God knew him, and he stood firmly on that. But now he was being mocked by those who once marveled at and were encouraged by his relationship with God. It was disheartening for Job. He urged his friends to look around at all of God's creation, and see whether they would testify of His goodness. The scripture says, "Who knoweth not in all these that the hand of the Lord hath wrought [accomplished] this? Whose hand is the soul of every living thing, and the breath of all mankind" (Job 12:9–10).

28

God was absolutely of great wisdom and strength, which none could contend. He held in His hand both the one who deceives and the deceived, both the oppressed and the oppressor. Job knew exactly who God was, the Creator of heaven and earth!

By this time Job was really agitated with his friends. He was tired of them putting him down and speaking to him as an ignorant and foolish man. Job, again, was "the greatest of all the men of the east" (Job 1:3). Considering the pedestal God placed Job on before Satan, Job was very special in God's eyes. His friends stood flat footed on their beliefs, thinking Job was lying and covering up something he had done. Job placed their value at zero, as worthless physicians, and he in turn called them liars (Job 13:4). He was tired of being blamed and falsely accused for what he was suffering. Job urged them to shut up and truly listen to his plight.

In so many words, Job posed a question: would they stand as God and wrongfully answer him in His stead? Job wondered: if God were to search their hearts, what would He find? Since they seemed to be perfect and have so much insight on Job's situation and the reason for his suffering, what would God say about them? If God confronted them, would they be standing so innocently and faultlessly, pointing fingers? Job was a man, just as they were, and

"Will ye speak wickedly for God? and talk deceitfully for Him?"
Job 13:7

he wanted them to grasp that. He said, "Hold your peace, and let me alone, that I may speak, and let come on me what will. Wherefore do I take my flesh in my teeth, and put my life in mine hand?" (Job 13:13–14). Job was simply tired and fed up.

Battle of Strength

Job then said (which is most believers' favorite quote and verse), "Though He slay me, yet will I trust in Him" (Job 13:15a). As I think about the many people/believers who love and quote this verse, I wonder, do they know the rest of it? The latter half of verse 15b says, "but I will maintain mine own ways before Him." While Job was encouraging himself, he also stood firmly, still, on his innocence— talk about the battle of strength. On one hand, Job said he will trust God no matter what, even in the midst of feeling like God was destroying him. Then, he spoke that he refused to change his stance before God.

Like Job, many of us speak boldly that we will trust God beyond our understanding, especially when we quote half of verse 15 and get so encouraged. We are so bold, and often give God our <u>best</u> praise after quoting the first half of the verse, but our actions confirm more so the lost and unknown end of the verse. We walk away after our praise and encouragement and do our own thing. We don't change a thing. Then we wonder why our lives and situations haven't changed. Just like we halfway read and quote this scripture, we halfway follow up on the things that require us to open our eyes and change what we have grown so familiar with. We say that we trust God with our entire heart, but we are holding so tightly to it because we unconsciously believe we know what is best for us. We believe God unjustly allows trouble into our lives. And instead of leaning and depending on Him to bring a resolve, our actions show the latter part of verse 15: "but I will maintain my own ways before Him."

Thereafter, Job's prayers were for God to take His hand from him so that he may be free, and to help him not be afraid of Him. These two requests were his constant prayers; he just wanted relief and peace from his affliction. Job pleaded with God to talk to him, promising to answer—or to just allow him an opportunity to speak that He may reply. Job's questions continued, becoming redundant. He asked God to enlighten him of the iniquities He was holding over his head. Job wondered if he was now reaping the consequences for what he had done in his younger years. Job was completely puzzled—he had no idea of the origin of his suffering. He felt like

God was holding him in contempt, with his hands and feet bonded with chains.

Job looked to God and expressed his hope that He would hear his cry. Then, Job looked at the trees and made a point about their life. If they were cut down, though their roots were very old, they would become strong again with just the fresh fragrance of water. A tree has hope to live again, but a man does not. Once he dies, there is no more life that could be expected. Despite this, Job believed there were brighter days ahead. He desired for God to cover him and hide him until his time of suffering was over. He wanted to be treated as a tree, if you will. He wanted God to give him rest, but he did not want God to forget about him (Job 14:7–13).

"For Thou writest bitter things against me, and makest me to possess the iniquities of my youth."
Job 13:26

Job knew when his change and his better days arrived, God would then have a need for him. His life would be worth living again. He recognized he had to wait for that day to come, and he was momentarily encouraged to keep holding on.

Although he waited for this revival wholeheartedly, he could not ignore the turmoil he was currently experiencing. Job knew God was watching his every move and did not blink at the sins he committed. Job explained that he believed God was holding on to all his iniquities and storing them up. Every evil thing he had ever done, he believed that God was remembering at this time. As sure as the mountains one day become nothing and as the waters destroy the rocks that dwell in it, so ". . . Thou destroyeth the hope of man" (Job 14:19). Job strongly felt as if God found pleasure in causing such misery and death upon man—upon him. Job was hurting and felt betrayed by his God.

"If a man dies, shall he live again? All the days of my appointed time will I wait, till my change come."
Job 14:14

Job 13:15 was at the core of Job's heart. Even through all the turmoil, pain, and confusion, he was determined to keep believing in God and pleading with Him. He was determined to stay before God, expressing his truths of how he felt. Job wasn't giving up. Job understood that his heart was sure before God; he wasn't a hypocrite, for they couldn't stand before God. He was certain his plea would be heard and justified. In this place, I believe Job's faith was increased and his hope rekindled, even as his stance on his innocence remained immovable.

Bildad and Zophar spoke to Job very confidently, just as Eliphaz did. They knew God to be who they knew Him to be, and Job the same. Job continued to fight, with the little strength he had left, to prove he was blameless and had received all this torture unjustly— which didn't faze his friends one bit. Job's friends refused to think any other way about what they understood. Bottom line: God is not a liar; Job had to be.

Yet, Job still did not curse God! God's word concerning Job was being upheld through the measure of grace God had given him.

CHAPTER 4

Second Speeches:
No Mercy
No Compassion
(Job 15-21)

Eliphaz and Job

Eliphaz confronted Job yet again. He rebuked Job for thinking he was wiser than everyone. In my understanding of Eliphaz's point of view, Job made himself look more foolish rather than bring clarity to his side of the story. Eliphaz believed Job discredited himself with his own words, and seemed agitated by Job's stance. Additionally, Eliphaz was confident that Job no longer feared God nor yielded to Him in prayer.

They did not perceive how Job, the youngest of the four, could possibly know the ways of God on a deeper level than they did. Their fathers were older and wiser, implying that Eliphaz, Bildad, and Zophar were bound to be taught with a greater wisdom. Very puzzled, Eliphaz asked Job: how could he carelessly speak so harshly, knowing that God was listening to everything he spoke? He seemed irritated and greatly offended by the expression of Job's pain and his confidence in the way he walked before God. He declared how evil and ordinary Job was; there was not anything special about him. Job's friends didn't believe he was greater and should be esteemed higher than they were. They simply claimed to be wiser.

Job was constantly defending his righteousness. Because his friends continued to accuse him, he got angry and began to point fingers at them. While they were all adamant of his guilt and immorality, Eliphaz's words and judgments were crucial. He said to Job: it is a known fact that the wicked would not be wealthy and everything that man acquired wouldn't last (Job 15:29). The hypocrites would certainly be abandoned and forsaken. The evil places where they dwelled would be devoured by a consuming fire.

> *"For the congregation of hypocrites shall be desolate, and fire shall consume the tabernacles of bribery."*
> *Job 15:34*

Eliphaz, just as Job, refused to back down from his very own wisdom and understanding.

35

Job's friends, he exclaimed, were a horrible support system. They did not know what to say out of their mouths. They were all too wise for their own good. They were too knowledgeable to just be quiet and let God do whatever He was doing. Somehow, they had to make a little bit of sense of it all. In this place, God wanted Job to know Him on a more personal level. _God wanted Job and his friends to know that He could not only protect them from evil and sickness, but He could also allow those things into their lives and also bring them through it much better than when they went in_. God desired to prove to them that He was more than just who they had grown to know Him to be, through their fathers and the generations that preceded them.

"I have heard many such things: miserable comforters are ye all."
Job 16:2

In their quest to find the mystery of Job's suffering, they were tearing him down, causing him more grief than when they arrived at his home. Job wondered how long they were going to keep running their mouths and putting forth false accusations. He questioned their motivations to keep arguing. Job asked, where was their boldness coming from?

Job said that if the roles were reversed, he would not treat them the way they were treating him. He would have compassion rather than speak words that would only make things worse. He would encourage them and use his wisdom to help them get through such grief, and not add to it.

"Shall vain words have an end? Or what emboldeneth thee that thou answereth?"
Job 16:3

Job realized his pain wasn't going to be relieved whether he expressed it or kept silent. But if Job had remained quiet, he would have been even more devastated. _His pain would have been greater had he internalized his emotions._

36

Humiliation in Exchange for Humility
Job and God

Furthermore, Job spoke to God about how forsaken he felt. Just as fast as he'd had a bit of hope, now he was in pain all over again. In Job chapter 14, Job was encouraged and strengthened, yet still crying out. But in chapter 15, Job was totally distraught again. He believed God hated him and had fixed His eyes on him, adding to his misery. Job says, "God hath delivered me to the ungodly, and turned me over into the hands of the wicked." (Job 16:11)

Job had been living a peaceful life before all this suffering came about. As Job saw it, God broke him and humiliated him for no cause. He was constantly crying and in despair—mostly due to his lack of understanding. Had he understood, he would have been able to wait it all out with a different fighting stance. Job's prayers were honest and unpolluted towards God. His hands were clean of all violence and offense. He was certain that his witness of his innocence was in heaven. He stood immovable on his reputation and the life he lived before God and man. His friends mocked him, but he was determined to keep crying out to God. He was sure the affliction he was made to endure would come to an end, one way or another.

The way Job handled everything is similar to my life. One moment he was hopeful; the very next, he was tormented by his pain and surroundings. One moment he wanted to die and wanted God to just leave him alone; the next moment, he was empowered to go on. One moment he was strengthened; then he was very much weakened. Through many things in my life I have had to bear, I too have experienced the same ups and downs. Because my service and dedication was sure, I ignorantly felt as if I didn't deserve any pain or lack. I believed, because of my "three grains of mustard seed" faith and level of understanding, I should have been further along than many, even those in my own family. There were definitely a few enlarged cells of pride there that weren't at all justified. I believed because God had this special love for me and because I loved Him, I shouldn't have to experience certain troubles and hardship. I simply should not have had to endure experiences that weren't easy to conquer. Even though I was serving God faithfully, and doing what I was taught in honoring God to the best of my ability, I still wasn't at a place in my relationship with Him where I completely <u>knew</u> Him.

Job, too, wasn't yet at a place of having the level of relationship with God that God was calling him to. Aside from the offerings made and the ways he was taught to fear and honor God, there was more God wanted from their relationship. To accomplish such a relationship desired by God, suffering was the road to be traveled. It was Job's time to be drawn even closer to God. He was already named "perfect and upright, and one that feared God . . ." (Job 1:1), without this deeper love for God. However, God decided it was time to rise to another level of closeness.

Can you imagine how sure God was about Job's footing in Him, and how much He loved Job? God was pleased with Job, even in this time of suffering and misery. God knew Job wasn't just doing as he was told by his forefathers. He knew Job meant his sacrifices and truly embedded all he had learned about Him in his heart. God loved Job! Job loved God! Job's love for God was unshakable, pure, and innocent. In all this turmoil and confusion, Job was trying his best to stay afloat and apply all the things he knew about God to sustain him.

"If I wait, the grave is mine house: I have made my bed in darkness."
Job 17:13

As Job finished up this response to his friend, he was very sorrowful. Again, Job attacked the wisdom of his friends because they had proven to him that they were foolish. And Job continued to rest in the "hope" of death and freedom from his misery.

Although Job believed he was innocent, he also believed that he had done something wrong. He was aware something wasn't one hundred percent right, which is why he continued to talk to God. He understood that the only one who could answer him, and make complete sense of all he was facing, was his God. Let me remind you: Job hadn't called his friends to help him in any way. His friends came on their own once they heard the news that was spread around the land. In my opinion, it could have been a nosy gesture. Were they jealous of him because he was named the greatest in the east? Were they only coming to see if their greatest competition had really and finally "fallen"?

Bildad and Job

In Bildad's second speech he confronted Job again and without compassion. Why would Job think he was so special, believing the rules would be altered for him? Why did Job look at his friends as the enemy: as those who desired to harm him?

Why, Bildad wondered, were they now considered to be so foul and offensive? They were just trying to help. Job's friends were ignoring or disregarding everything he was saying to defend himself. Was Job's disposition to blame? Job, of course, was expressing all types of emotions: anger, sadness, desperation, peace, joy, and misery. Was this our perfect friend, Job?

> *"Yea, the light of the wicked shall be put out, and the spark of his fire shall not shine."*
> *Job 18:5*

Bildad was not easing up on his accusations. Like Job, he was confident in his wisdom. He spoke of more consequences for the wicked: they'd continue to dwell in the darkness, and their light would surely be blown out!

Bildad did not pay attention to Job's heart and frustrations. It seemed as if everyone was defending themselves, standing on their own valid truths. No one was open to being corrected. Once again, they were all too wise for a situation such as this. It was unlike any other situation they had ever heard about or seen. Everyone wanted to be right because of their stature, and who they were known to be individually.

Bildad disregarded Job's credibility. Even if Job had made only one mistake, Bildad and his friends took Job's present suffering as him living a lie all of his years. They truly believed that Job was a hypocrite. As his friends understood, Job was now reaping what he had sown under the mask of a perfect life. This whole situation was beyond their comprehension and wisdom; they could not have known. Or could they have known? Had they slowed down their accusations, spoke less, and prayed more, they could have known and gained some wisdom from the Giver of wisdom. James 1:5 says, "If any man lack wisdom, let him ask of God, that giveth to all men liberally, and upbraideth not; and it shall be given him."
Amen.

Was Job Abandoned by God?

Job asked Eliphaz, Bildad, and Zophar, "How long will ye vex my soul, and break me in pieces with your words?" (Job 19:2). Simply put, he asked why they were still there. They were just causing him greater distress on top of the evident afflictions he already had to bear. Job, again, expressed that God was destroying him and entangling him in a net of sorrow. He cried aloud to God, but neither He nor anyone else came to his rescue. Job was so distraught!

From what Job comprehended of the thoughts racing through his mind, he had been abandoned by God. Job was very confused and hopeless. He was an enemy of God. Job had also been alienated by his family and closest friends, those who'd always been around. His maids and servants didn't pay him any attention. He would call for them and they would ignore him. How low and depressing is that? Perhaps they were no longer around because he had nothing more to give. How worthless did he feel at that moment in his life? His family and those who were usually around were all gone. No one was acknowledging him in the darkest days of his life. Yes, three of his friends were there, but they were not helping him at all. They were carrying him closer and closer to the edge of the cliff, encouraging him to leap.

In his most crucial time, all those who were so familiar to Job—when he was on top and prosperous—were now gone. Even his wife treated him as a stranger (Job 19:17). Job lost more than just his children, substance, and his good health; Job was facing death already. Then, his so-called wise friends bashed him and afflicted more discouragement, sadness, and anguish, killing him with every word they spoke. Job was in an impossible place, yet he never cursed God. Though he spoke harshly, God understood and forgave him. Job never crossed that line. Job was strong per the measure given to him to survive.

"He hath stripped me of my glory and taken my crown from my head."
Job 19:9

God knew he could handle this! Job was the 'good talk' of the east before all this suffering had befallen him. Everyone preferred him, yet now in his misery, while he was hurting, no one wanted anything to do with him. He had encouraged and helped a countless number of people. But now that he had suffered the loss of his children and all his wealth, and was fighting for his life and hope, he was as the dirt of the earth. Job's value seemed to be his things. It was what he could offer the people from his substance. That is so low!

Job was aggravated and disappointed by his friends, and pleaded with them to stop adding to his pain; he had enough from what God was allowing. Even in all of this, Job spoke that his hope was no more, yet he had a hope and faith in God that ran much deeper than his mere words. This hope and faith ran deeper than the pain he felt and he tried his best to express it clearly, without cursing God. Job was confident that his Redeemer was yet alive. His hope truly rested in seeing God one day, after his suffering was long over (Job 19:25–26).

While Job was hopeful about seeing God face to face after death, he warned his friends to be afraid of the judgment they'd receive if they kept focusing on the reason he was being afflicted. Job admonished them that it was certain to come, and would be undeniable when they saw God on that day. Job tried to open their eyes to see that God's judgment reached everyone: they weren't exempt. He wanted them to stop focusing so much on his current condition and worry about what judgment they'd receive themselves.

> *"Be ye afraid of the sword: for wrath bringeth the punishments of the sword, that ye may know there is a judgment."*
> Job 19:29

Zophar and Job

Zophar, during his last speech, was very angry with what Job was saying. He, too, refused to alter his conclusion of the matter: Job was wicked and deserved all he was getting from the hand of God. Zophar strongly disagreed with Job and did not hesitate to release his thoughts about it. Job was absolutely aware how things had been from the beginning of time. He knew that the wicked reigned for just a moment, and hypocrites experienced joy for only that same short moment; it did not last long at all. Today they were; tomorrow they would be washed away, withered like the grass.

Zophar wasn't cutting Job any slack. He knew Job was well learned in the ways of the land, which is where Zophar's defense was coming from. He then reiterated that everything that the wicked gained, God would cause them to lose. They would become sick and be forced to release all they had in their possession. There was

42

nothing the wicked could touch or do that would not come back to harm them. Zophar exclaimed, the wicked would not see the land of plenty where the waters were ever flowing: ". . . the brooks of honey and butter" (Job 20:17).

As to the hope that Job rested in and looked forward to, the brighter day he rejoiced in: Zophar implied that because of his wickedness, Job could forget about it. Those who were evil would not have peace but for a very small moment. Zophar wanted to make it clear to Job that because of his iniquities, the very iniquities he refused to confess, his dark days were now very deserved. As far as Zophar understood, Job was getting his just due. After this, Zophar had nothing else to say about it.

Job's disposition seemed much calmer—I can imagine how tired and depleted he must have been—but Job still had much to say to his friends. He encouraged his friends to listen closely, and thereafter answer as they pleased. Job said his complaints were not to mere men, who were simply incapable of helping him. He would have had every right to be sorrowful and perplexed, had that been the case(Job 21:4).

> **"The increase of his house shall depart, and his goods shall flow away in the day of his wrath."**
> **Job 20:28**

Job wondered, why shouldn't he be bothered by the suffering he had to bear? He was speaking and begging God to help him, yet He was not answering. Job believed he had every right to feel and express his confusion and his pain. His friends were a disgrace to him— worthless—as he had stated before. He was tired of dealing with them. He urged them to look at how bad his body had been afflicted, look at what he was going through. Job was disgusted and terrified at his own body, and he made it clear to them that there was a valid reason for his complaint and distress.

Why Are the Wicked Blessed?

During Job's trouble, he asked several questions to express himself and cause everyone to think. Why did the wicked live to be so old and seem to hold so much power, and why were they prosperous? Why was God dealing so graciously with them? Even their families were blessed—happy and full of life. Job knew the hearts of the wicked rejected God and all His ways, yet they were not made to suffer. He was completely baffled at the thought—how could they be so evil yet so blessed?

"What is the Almighty, that we should serve Him? And what profit should we have, if we pray unto Him?"
Job 21:15

Job went on and asked: what does a man gain if he serves and honors God? If the wicked were blessed to prosper, even if just for a moment, what made us different if we're submitting to the hand of God? The evildoer's prosperity was God's doing, not their own. Job certainly believed and said confidently that he was not among those who refuse to fear God; he was not evil. Job placed himself in a category far different than the unjust. His confusion and frustration derived from the fact that God rewarded both those who purposed in their heart to honor Him and those who chose not to.

Job was righteous, he was innocent; he had no reason to believe otherwise because his deeds and lifestyle were undeniable before God and the people. Job expressed repeatedly that he did not deserve to be treated as the wicked when he had wholeheartedly served God and sacrificed before Him. How could Job possibly understand how he could be compared to such evil when he lived an upright and perfect life?

"Lo, their good is not in their hand: the counsel of the wicked is far from me."
Job 21:16

All things considered, Job was hurting so badly. Job questioned who could know the depths of God; He who would allow one to die who was perfectly healthy, and allow one to die who was ill. They both had a resting place in the grave, and they both turned to dust in the end. Job just did not understand the extent of God's wisdom. He was confident in what he knew, but it was all surface-level understanding compared to the infinite wisdom and understanding of God.

Job articulated to his friends that he was well aware of the negative thoughts that they had toward him. The thoughts: how could Job say he was so righteous, yet now resemble those who were wicked? Job's friends stated in so many words that it was a clear distinction between the righteous and the wicked.

"They shall lie down alike in the dust, and the worms shall cover them."
Job 21:26

Job's response to their negative disposition: God was who possessed all the evidence of who was who, the righteous and the wicked. He would repay those who were wicked in their hearts, and He would reward the righteous accordingly. But just as the wicked experienced death, so did those who lived a life honorable before God. How could man know the things that were only certain to God?

Job felt betrayed at his friends' view of him and how they received the things he spoke. He was truly hurt and never imagined he would have to endure such agony. Though devastated, he still desired that his friends comprehend, once again, that even though he was suffering so much pain, which seemed like the reward of the wicked; God reigned over all and knew all. Though he was in great despair and he didn't feel he justly deserved to be under the same umbrella as the hypocrites, he still fought for his sanity and his innocence. Job was torn and disappointed at the lack of support and comfort from his friends. Their answers, even in this moment, weren't at all encouraging or lifting him out of his darkness. Neither mercy nor compassion was given to Job in his most devastating place. Eliphaz, Bildad, and Zophar were only driving daggers of heartache and depression into his heart.

In all this despair, pain, anger, and uncertainty expressed, it wasn't written that Job cursed God.

CHAPTER 5

Eliphaz & Bildad:
Stop Defending Yourself
(Job 22-27)

Eliphaz and Job

In Eliphaz's last speech, he began with a question to Job: what did God get out of making him righteous? He intended to plead with Job, encouraging him to repent and get back on the right track. He expressed to Job everything he believed he had done in his past that caused him to reap such punishment. According to Eliphaz, Job ignored the widows and treated the less fortunate poorly. He wondered, was God causing Job to suffer because he was righteous? Eliphaz continued to stress to Job that he was not innocent.

Eliphaz's Contradiction

According to Eliphaz, Job had taken things from people for his own financial gain. He walked past and ignored those who were hungry, even though he had the means to help them (Job 21:7).

Eliphaz exclaimed that Job was the wealthiest man, yet he was selfish and stingy. He held back giving his money that he may continue to prosper and he did not attempt to help the ones who were fatherless. Eliphaz accused Job of these horrible things, and said it was why a great suffering was placed upon him. He could not understand why Job was so blind to all of his iniquities [sins].

If we go back to Eliphaz's first speech, we will see how Eliphaz was now contradicting himself, unless he was speaking sarcastically. In the fourth chapter of Job, Eliphaz spoke about Job being a great help to so many people. He encouraged and strengthened them when they were in need. When those who were weak sought out Job, he was there to comfort them. Bottom line: when people asked Job for any type of assistance, he came to their aid. He was known for it *(Job 4:3–4)*.

But now, to prove Job was full of iniquity, Eliphaz, his friend, was saying something totally different. His desire was to enlighten Job of his mistakes and where he failed in God's sight. Was Eliphaz finally breaking down the truth of how Job operated—this perfect and respectable man whom God had boasted about and served on a silver platter before Satan? Was this God, who was so faithful and true, now made a liar by this wise friend of Job's? What was really going on at this point?

Although Eliphaz was still accusing Job of so much evil, he seemed to have calmed down from his second speech to help Job "get it right." He was desperately trying to get Job to admit his wrongs, so his affliction could be over. I understood Eliphaz to be coming from a more concerned and desperate standpoint to assist Job in realizing his faults.

Eliphaz then encouraged Job to repent for all the wicked things he had done; to just apologize to God and watch Him turn it all around. If Job truly desired peace, his only way to that destination was to confess to God and allow God to renew him.

Eliphaz strongly expressed that if Job was to pray to God with a repentant heart, God would hear him. God would hear Job's renewed vows and honor him; God would simply smile on Job yet again. If Job would just humble himself in such a way, God would restore him. Through Job's repentance and humility, he would cause others, who were unrighteous, to be saved and delivered. Eliphaz was now insistently pleading with Job to turn it all around through simply giving up the blanket that was covering his iniquities. Eliphaz encouraged Job that it was not too late, he was not yet too far gone (Job 22:25–26).

"Thou shalt make thy prayer unto Him, and He shall hear thee, and thou shalt pay thy vows."
Job 22:27

Job's Confidence on Display

Job was still in great despair, and his words were only those of grief. His constant crying and moaning had not eased the weight that

50

God had allowed to consume him. He was desperate to find God and to hear what He had to say in response to the matters of his heart. Job was confident that God would not turn His back on him. In that place where God rested, Job knew God heard the voice of those who were righteous and that He would deliver them. Job longed to dwell where God was, but Job could not find Him.

Rather than be completely discouraged, Job was encouraged in that very moment. He couldn't find God, but he was confident that God knew exactly where he was.

Even through this terrible time in Job's life, God knew where Job was and Job refused to believe otherwise. Job understood at this moment that he was going to come out of this fire shining bright, gleaming as pure gold. He would be better than when he entered his suffering. Job's hope was yet again rekindled in the heart of his misery. <u>Though he did not see God or hear Him, he knew God was watching over him.</u>

"But He knoweth the way that I take: when He hath tried me, I shall come forth as gold."
Job 23:10

Job stood on his relationship with God. He did not allow his friends to make him second guess his track record and the life he lived. Job honored God and followed His commandments, and his steps never rejected God's way. He did not go against what God spoke to him. He obeyed God and desired God's Word, far more than his desire for natural food (Job 23:12).

Was Job Prideful?
Once again, Job expressed, God was sovereign and He would do whatever He wanted to do. Whatever God desired to allow him or anybody else to experience He would surely allow. For this reason, Job was afraid of what more God would take him through, since where he stood was extremely tortuous. Job's heart was troubled and

51

made faint by the things God allowed, but he understood that the fight was not yet over. He had no clue what more to expect and he was terrified because of it.

Job continued to wonder about God's judgment concerning the wicked. He asked, why didn't God immediately punish those who would steal from the poor? All those wicked people who oppressed those less fortunate, took from the hungry, and treated people and animals with cruelty: why did not God charge them with all the suffering he was experiencing? Those who were stripping people of their clothes, causing them to struggle in the bitter cold and to find shelter wherever they may: where was their judgment? (Job 24:8).

The oppressors took children from their mothers. They made the poor communities work hard for them, yet they did not feed them nor pay them enough in exchange. The poor and the afflicted cried out for help because of the wicked who caused them to suffer. Job, being innocent and honest, did not understand or think it was fair that they were not made to suffer, but he was (Job 24:19).

Perhaps, in this moment, Job found more strength and hope in acknowledging the definite end of the wicked, knowing that was not his end because of his good reputation and righteousness.

God always watched those who had done evil, and their temporary rest would soon be interrupted. Without any doubt, their exalted place would be brought down very low. Job knew this to be true because he lived by the law of God. Though he seemed a bit exalted himself, his lifestyle supported the very things he spoke. This was all he could lean on and this supported his strong disposition and his hope.

As I continued to explore Job's character, I found that pride was associated with it. In Job 24:25 he says, "And if it be not so now, who will make me a liar, and make my speech nothing worth [worth

52

nothing]?"

Job didn't see how he could be challenged, because he had been walking with God for such a long time, not to mention because of who he was known to be. Instead of allowing there to be an opportunity and space for humility, Job stood incomparable and took another step up on his ladder.

No matter what we feel and how sure we are about a subject matter, humility is always necessary. Yes, Job was frustrated at his "unjust" sufferings and the hand he'd been dealt, but Job needed to remain careful of how he spoke and expressed himself. Throughout all of this it is evident that he didn't curse God, but his words became very harsh at times. Though we are human, allowed to feel and express our hurt and frustrations, we must still be conscious of not becoming so engulfed in our pain that we step up on a high horse, believing we are ever above our current situation. We are never greater than what God has allowed, and we are to remain humble knowing that God will give us the strength, grace, and wisdom needed to overcome and pull through.

I take this to heart and will govern myself accordingly. Through Job's story I see more and more of myself—sometimes believing I am above chastisement and correction. Even when we think we are above reproof, we need to stop, drop, and re-evaluate. The only one who isn't worthy of reproof and judgment is God. Let's remove that pride and stop focusing so much on what everybody else is doing wrong, and what judgment they ought to receive. Let's work on correcting our individual issues and imperfections.

At one time in my life, there were a lot of people I ignorantly thought I was "above," or better than, because I lived the best I knew how by the Book: Word of God. By understanding where Job is in this text, it allows the light to shine on the beam in my own eye. Just because I may do what is required of me by the Word of God, to the best of my knowledge, does not at all mean that I am perfect. It doesn't mean I am in a place where I can compare others to myself, as if positioned to look down on them. From what I saw, I was "perfect" in my efforts to please God, striving to be honest and living honorably, and seemingly more serious than my neighbor about living a life satisfying to God. I loved God with all my heart, and I didn't <u>intentionally</u> do evil, but I wasn't—and I, absolutely, am not—faultless. I am human, born in sin and "shapen in iniquity . . ." as written in Psalms 51:5. God is the only One who is named faultless, just, righteous, and pure, without any assistance from another. He is the only One without sin, without any offense.

The question then becomes, what is in our members that is covered up by our good works? Excuse me—what is in *my* members that may be covered up by *my* good works? Why am I so dedicated to God? ...To keep me from what? What is God saving me from? What is the true deal about me?

Instead of trying to answer these questions for another person, we need to look inwardly and find out what impurities God is trying to get rid of. We should individually search out "what is in me that is not quite mirroring the image and likeness that I was created in?" (Genesis 1:26). We have to get the beam out of our own eye so we can see clearly. Don't worry about the wicked and their reward. Focus on what you are doing and why God has allowed suffering to come your way.

Bildad and Job

Bildad's final speech was simply put. He stated, in very few words, that only God could know the meaning of all that had befallen Job. He's above all, and the wisest. God held complete dominion and honor; who could know all of those who contend for God? (Job 25:2).

How Could Job Stand So Confident?

Bildad exclaimed that man was nothing more than a useless slimy worm that was nourished from dead bodies; God was greater than any other. But Bildad quickly gave up the fight because he saw he could not convince Job that he was guilty. Bildad understood that neither he nor any other man was as wise as God. He accepted the fact that he could not figure out this great mystery that rested in the bosom of God concerning Job. He asked Job, how could man be pure before God? He could not fathom man being labeled as righteous and blameless. It was seemingly impossible. In this moment, Bildad was not only speaking for all men created, but especially Job (Job 25).

Job got a little more agitated with Bildad and his other friends. Bildad had not brought clarity for Job at all. He had failed to help Job in finding rest and peace about his situation. Job was weak and his friends had failed terribly at pouring life into him. They had given poor counsel to Job, who was already perplexed and troubled, in spirit and in body. Job wondered: what kind of spirit was leading them to "help" him? He concluded that they could not have been guided by the spirit of God because they spoke with neither wisdom, compassion, nor mercy.

Job's friends weren't giving sound counseling to pick Job up out of his dark place. Just as Bildad mentioned, man wasn't much more than a worm. Well, Job believed Eliphaz, Bildad, and Zophar were worthy of that comparison. Job made it known to them, again, that they were worthless, and that they'd offered the worst advice that any man could be given in such a miserable and depressing place. Job was offended by Bildad's words because, as we all know, Job confidently claimed he was without fault. Bildad firmly going against what Job believed frustrated Job. No matter what, Job stood by his faithful and consistent lifestyle. He was not shaken!

Job then, in detail, illustrated the greatness of God and all God had done from the moment He spoke, "Let there be light" (Genesis 1:3). Job expressed how God spoke life into an empty and void space, and how from a mere word everything was created.

"He stretcheth out the north over the empty place, and hangeth the earth upon nothing."
Job 26:7

Job articulated God's awesome works: the heavens and the earth and many of the things that dwell therein. Though Job laid out a great deal of the mighty things God had done, he noted that he had only scratched the surface of who God was and what He could do (Job 26:14).

As has been noted, God was so mighty that He knew what was in the heights of the heavens and the depths of the earth. Nothing was hidden from His sight. God was simply great and incomparable. Even though Job stood strongly on his innocence, he could not ignore the might and mystery of God; he had grown very familiar with it. Job was endeavoring to open his friends' eyes that they may know that he was aware that God was the Almighty. He wanted them to know that he not only knew God, but also that no one could contain all His great wisdom. God was truly above all! He knew the ins and outs of all things, good and evil.

Job's friends' desire was for him to give up the fight. They wanted Job to lose his confidence, but Job refused, time and time again. His strength rested in what he had become familiar with; his fear and reverence of God developed from their relationship. No matter what, Job's confidence couldn't be shaken by his friends. It continued to grow stronger and stronger.

And Job still did not curse God.

CHAPTER 6

Job Speaks:
Where Is My God?
(Job 27-31)

Job's Final Expression of Frustration

Job continued to express his point of view to his friends, and at some points to God. He mentioned that God was the One with the power and authority to challenge and strip him of his righteousness—of his clean slate—and cause great pain to the core of his soul. Although God orchestrated Job's suffering, Job still vowed that he would only speak what was holy and righteous. Job was making a declaration, a promise to God, speaking with great assurance on where he stood in his relationship with God. He was not going to speak evil of God or against God just because he had to bear such "undeserved" pain. While he still had breath in his body, he would hold onto his integrity, which God spoke of when Satan came to Him the second time. Job could not turn from God because he would then be the hypocrite he said he was not, making his friends' claims accurate.

Job knew that the wicked prevailed for only a moment. They had no hope, and God would not hear their cry. Job was determined to rehearse to his friends all that he knew concerning the ways of God, even though they themselves had witnessed it already. They were acting as if they were unlearned, through their conversations and "comforting" attempts. Job went on to explain, again, that the wicked would not prosper, and they would receive their just due at the hand of God. Their children would die at the sword and suffer hunger, as they have made others suffer. They would lack greatly. They would work hard to gain the riches of this world, only to see it laid up for the righteous. The wicked would be overtaken. They were going to get back what they had put out (Job 27:21).

Searching for Wisdom

Job described the many different treasures God enabled man to seek out and obtain. God had not hidden gold and silver so deep within the earth that man could not find it. He did not hide the treasures of the earth in a place where it could not be sought out— be it food or valuables found in the depths of the sea and at the bottom of the mountains. He allowed us the luxury and blessing of searching for and finding precious stones, crystals, onyx, sapphires, and gold. God allowed us to search out and find valuable metals such as brass and iron, which are hidden treasures of the earth. There were other treasures hidden in the earth that lions and fowls of the air could never lay hold to, but God granted man the strength to seek them out and obtain them (Job 28:1–10).

Moreover, in Job 28:12, Job says, "But where shall wisdom be found? And where is the place of understanding?" There was one thing that Job's soul was searching for that was not hidden in the depths of the sea and at the bottom of the mountains. This treasure, whose value was truly unmatched, was not hidden in the earth as the other precious gems and valuable stones. Its value: priceless!

Job knew where to go to find riches and treasures of the earth, but what he longed for was not so easily captured! It was not found among pearls or coral, or even pure gold; it was incomparable to those precious gems and stones, by far!

In Job 28:18 it says, "for the price of wisdom is above rubies." Job was seeking out wisdom and understanding. He knew it was resting in heavenly places; it wasn't among the living on earth, and it didn't rest where the birds could reach and obtain it.

Only God knew where wisdom and understanding dwelled. Once again, God was above all and saw all. Who else could we look to, to find a treasure of priceless value? God directs the lightning and the thunder; He measures how much it will rain. That's the power and might He contain.

The omnipresent God, looking over all the earth, and in the heavens, saw wisdom and named it. He prepared it for His children; He searched it out and made it available to us, that we may know Him (Job 28:27).

Furthermore, it was explained that wisdom is to honor and respect God, and understanding is to be separated from sin and wickedness (Job 28:28).

Even in these words spoken clearly by God, there is a mystery. We must seek God for such treasure! There is no other way to obtain such.

Job Lost His Honor

Job began to look back over his life prior to the suffering of his today. He longed to experience those days again. In those days, God had smiled on him and was pleased with him. In those days, Job rested in the peace and protection of God (Job 29:4). Job was remembering when he and his whole household were blessed by God.

Job made clear to his friends who he was known to be in all the land, and the many works he had done. Again, Job decided to lay out how valuable and important he was to all people, especially those in need. He shared how no one spoke ill of him and respected him to the utmost. The people had honored him and the life he lived. As mentioned before, he had tended to those in need: the fatherless, the poor, the blind, the lame, and the widows. He, too, expressed how those on their deathbed blessed him for all he had done for them. Job was great to all people!

Job said in Job 29:14, "I put on righteousness and it clothed me: my judgment was a robe and a diadem." Simply put, Job did what was right! He treated all those that crossed his path with love and without partiality. Job thought that, because of these righteous deeds, he would have been granted a peaceful and honorable death.

The masses had heard Job. Every word he spoke they gave ear to and listened to very diligently. No one had doubted him or revolted

61

against him to challenge him. They heard his counsel; he was sought after for such. The people had openly received him, as the earth receives the rain. Even though there were some who did not believe in him, it did not steal his joy: the glory of the Lord continued to rest on him. Job had led the people and sat as a king among them. Job was the reason they knew of comfort and relief; he was their light and hope (Job 29:23).

Job was known as all these great things, but now things were different. God had allowed Satan to interrupt Job's life, as he knew it. Job was not so great anymore. He was now dwelling in the humiliation of his suffering; no one honored him anymore. Job felt just as low, if not lower, than those who he had once helped. They were now laughing at and mocking him. Those younger than Job were now disrespecting him, pointing fingers at him. Their fathers were men Job would have categorized with dogs; that was how low Job saw them. These men were cast out into the streets and shunned by others, as if they were thieves, but now Job was being mocked by them. Job was devastated at the reality of it all. These people were shunning him and spitting in his face as if oblivious to all he had done for them in the past.

"They abhor me, they flee far from me, and spare not to spit in my face."
Job 30:10

God had allowed Job to be afflicted; the people whom Job used to help and protect were now rejecting and disrespecting him. They were attacking him, which they'd never done before. How could those who'd had hope in Job keep their hope, when he didn't seem to possess it? The hope Job used to speak about seemed to have failed him. So why would they continue to honor him and look towards him for anything? Job didn't have anything else to give the people and his words were no longer comforting. Now, he was nothing more than who they were.

It's unbelievable how things had now turned around for Job. When someone is on top and doing exceptionally well, everyone honors them and crowds them for what they have and can offer. But as soon as they begin to suffer and lose all they were once handing out, there is no one in sight to help them. It is very sad. It also illustrates how unhealthy communities behave. Instead of working together to lift each other up, especially those who once lent a helping hand, they tend to kick each other while they're down and separate themselves. <u>Why is it that some only grow in their own hearts to make sure only they survive, rather than grow in the capacity to encourage and strengthen someone else?</u> Job's friends in his old community—the wise and wealthy—beat him down. When Job became part of the poor community, they did the same, kicking him and spitting in his face. There was no hope to be found anywhere in Job's most difficult place, yet Job never cursed God.

On top of all this despair, Job was crying out to God and God still hadn't replied to him. Perhaps, as I've mentioned before, if God had spoken to him, he would've had some level of relief and peace, helping him to hang in there. He was in great pain, and still had no answer from who he trusted in and depended on the most. God wasn't acknowledging Job at all, but some of us know the plot: God was there the entire time. He was watching his every move and listening to his every word.

Job cried out to God amid his destruction and affliction, but God never said a word. Job was confused. How was it that he did all these things to help the poor and wipe the tears of the weary, yet evil was his reward? He had no rest; his pain did not provide for such. He cried out to his community, but no one acknowledged him. His cry was now like a screeching bird. His skin was peeling and his body was tormented with fevers. The joyful melody that once came from his voice was now the sound of distressful wailing (Job 30:25–31).

Job continued to justify himself in the last bit of his speech. As we already understand, Job was adamant about his righteous life. He never let it go. Perhaps if he had, he may have given up long before this point. Job trusted that he never crossed the vow he held before God. He was certain that everyone knew that he walked upright. He didn't have sexual encounters with any woman other than his wife. He expressed how God was a witness to all his works. He knew that God saw his every move and whether he lived an evil and wicked life or not.

If God saw otherwise than where Job placed his confidence, he wished that God would judge him accordingly. If Job was wrong, he begged for someone to enlighten him of such, if God still refused to speak to him. If Job had lusted after another woman, he said he would openly accept the consequences of his wife being given to other men. He understood the punishments of a sinful life, which was why he lived the way he lived before God, avoiding evil.

If he had mistreated the poor or even the fatherless, he wanted this to be clear, so he could understand the reason behind his sufferings. All in all, he wanted to right all of his wrongs. He knew if God confronted him of all the sins he had committed, he couldn't defend it: God knew all things. Job had a certain level of understanding of the ways of God, yet none of this was connected to all he had learned over the course of his life. Job was confident and sure that he was innocent and free of all offenses.

"Then let mine arm fall from my shoulder blade, and mine arm be broken from the bone."
Job 31:22

Job asked, "If I covered my transgressions as Adam, by hiding mine iniquity in my bosom . . ." (Job 31:33), what would be the

64

reason? Would it be for fear of how people would view him? Was he more afraid of what people would say rather than what God had to say? Bottom line, Job wanted to hear only God's judgment. He wanted to hear God's voice and His voice only. He wanted to hear all that the enemy (which Job now viewed as God) had recorded. Whatever was written he would cleave to it and wear it as a crown and let it rest on his shoulders, proudly. He would be glad to know the things written about him, and wear the crown that was rightfully his, be it evil or good (Job 31:35–36).

Job wanted the truth to be spoken of all he had done. If he had caused distress to his land, or if the people testified of sins he had committed, he wanted the punishments due to him. Job said that he would take the book before God as a prince and lay out every detail of his life. If Job had brought to God actions that didn't resemble righteousness and all that he was sure he stood on, he said, "Let thistles grow instead of wheat, and cockle [weeds] instead of barley" (Job 31:40).

Although he brought up all these "ifs," he was also proving to everyone that he was pure and righteous. He was putting before the people his innocence; he declared, again and again, that he wasn't evil. He wasn't making money his God, and he didn't lust after things or women. Had he done so, he would have placed fame and fortune above God—that was the heart of the wicked. Job didn't wish evil to come upon those who mistreated him; he didn't find any pleasure in seeing people chastised for their actions. He never cursed a person's soul, no matter what. Job had much regard for everyone. He even opened his house to strangers traveling by.

Job was positioning himself to accept the judgment of God, even though in his heart he knew and believed he was innocent and had done those things which were right in the sight of God.

Job was desperately waiting on God to simply answer him. He was very distraught and was seeking deeply for the voice of God. He was even asking God to send the answer through someone else, if He chose not to speak to him directly. Job was dissecting his life and the deeds he had done throughout, trying to find anything, literally anything, to explain what was going on in his life: why had God forsaken him. Job cried and prayed and sought answers every single moment of this devastating pain and affliction. Job was confused and frustrated, wondering more and more: "Where is my God?"

CHAPTER 7

Elihu Speaks:
Only God Is Righteous
(Job 32-37)

Elihu and Friends

Among Job and his three friends: Eliphaz, Bildad, and Zophar, was another man by the name of Elihu. He had been there the entire time as Job went back and forth with his friends. When Job's friends ran out of words to say, refusing to respond to him, Elihu finally spoke up. Although he was the youngest of them all, he was no doubt the wisest. When finally able to speak, he expressed that he was very upset because, although these men were older, they were not exemplifying it. Job's friends had decided not to answer him after his last response because it was understood that "he was righteous in his own eyes" (Job 32:1). Regardless of what they might say to him, he unapologetically refused to hear them. Elihu was also upset with Job because he was more focused on clearing his name of accusations rather than justifying God and proving God to be righteous.

". . . against Job was his wrath kindled, because he justified himself rather than God."
Job 32:2

Elihu, the youngest of the group, had been hesitant to speak because he had great respect for his elders. But once they became quiet and gave up the fight, the spirit inside of him stood up. God gave him wisdom and an understanding of the situation at hand. He understood that none of Job's friends had helped Job to see the root of his issue. Once Elihu began to speak to them, neither Job nor his friends bothered responding or interrupting.

He was led to confront them in a very direct and stern way without trying to appease their feelings. If he spoke with any partiality or consolation, God would have dealt with him accordingly. In other words, Elihu had to give them what God gave him, without taking away from it or adding to it. He feared God and was not stepping forward to stroke their egos or pacify them.

"Behold I am according to thy wish in God's stead: I also am formed out of the clay."
Job 32:6

With a pure heart and sincerity, the young man boldly confronted Job. He wanted Job to receive what he had to say, and to understand that he was only there to help him. He made it clear to Job that he did not need to be afraid of him, for Elihu was a man just like him. He was not greater than Job; he came in the name of the Lord.

God is Greater, Yet He Answers Man
Elihu and Job

Elihu stated in Job 33:12, "Behold in this thou art not just: I will answer thee, that God is greater than man." Having been present for the conversations, Elihu remembered Job often saying that God was unjust, and that He had dealt with him as His enemy. But what Job concluded was false. Although Job thought he was innocent, he definitely was not. Job constantly complained that God wouldn't answer him. Elihu said that God answers—but when He answered, Job may not have understood. It was explained that he could have missed the answer because his expectation was for God to speak in a specific way.

Elihu exclaimed there were two ways God spoke to man. According to the scripture, one way was through dreams and visions. In those dreams and visions, God would warn man of what would befall him if his ways did not change. In this way of speaking to man, it was explained that God was trying to protect him from sin and pride by giving instructions that he must follow. This was to save man from chastisement. Those instructions were given to keep man from the rash consequences of his mistakes, but he must listen and take heed.

"He keepeth back his soul from the pit, and his life from perishing by the sword."
Job 33:18

The other way God spoke to man, Elihu mentioned, was through sickness. In lieu of saving man from death, God would allow affliction and pain to the body (Job 33:19). It would be a pain so bad that it would restrict man to his bed, and the loss of strength and weight would cause his bones to be visible through his skin. In that place man would long for a natural death.

Elihu further explained, if there is an angel sent to minister to him in pursuit of turning him to God, man could be saved from destruction. The angel would stand in the gap and lead him to salvation that he may be in good standing with God. If he complies, he would be saved from destruction and his soul would be delivered from death. God would renew him and he would be more beautiful than before: a new creature. He would be able to pray to God and be heard of Him. God would see the reflection of His joy when He saw him and would <u>declare</u> him righteous, something man could never do in and of himself (Job 33:15–28).

God desired, even in the days of Job, to bring everyone who had fallen short back into good standing with Him. God didn't want man to dwell in darkness and reject Him. God has always loved man, His beloved creation; oftentimes, His heart was broken because man strayed from Him. God, even in the book of Job, had made a way for man to be reconciled back to Him after man had chosen to walk his own way. God saved man time and time again because of the love, forgiveness, and desire He had for us to dwell with Him. He didn't want anyone to perish or to be disconnected from Him. God wanted man, and the essence of man: his heart.

In this text explaining the ways God answered man, it is proven that He gave man chance after chance after chance to come back to Him. If man would just hear and submit to Him, man would be saved and delivered from the pains of this world. Therefore, man would then be unable to keep his testimony to himself of how God healed and delivered him—how God saved him from darkness—and how He granted him to live in the light of the glory of God by His unexplainable love (Job 33:28–30).

Furthermore, Elihu articulated to Job, God was the One who made one righteous, and it was by His hands only. God was the One who turned the life of a sinner around that they may live a more glorious and acceptable life unto Him (Job 33:30).

The young man encouraged Job to remain quiet and hear everything he had to say, but, if Job had anything to say to defend himself or clear anything up, Elihu was open to hear him out. He wanted to help Job understand everything spoken, so that Job could be freed. Elihu was there to give Job wisdom as God directed.

At this point, Elihu not only spoke directly to Job, but to his friends as well. In Job 34:7, Elihu asked, "What man is like Job, who drinketh up scorning like water?" He, again, urged them to listen very closely so that they may determine the truth of judgment and what was named good by the hand of God. He pointed out that Job was calling God a liar, indirectly. Pastor Alonzo M. Walker, Sr. (my former pastor) expressed, on many occasions: "we have good enough sense not to outright call God a liar", or speak against what we believe is unfair or unacceptable for what we are going through. Instead, we beat around the bush about what we believe and how we deal with that belief in our "justified," self-righteous, and ignorant ways.

As mentioned so many times, Job stood immovable on his innocence. Yet Elihu pointed out the things Job uttered which resembled the wicked. Job said a few times, "It profiteth a man nothing that he should delight [please] himself with God" (Job 34:9). This proved that Job spoke as an unrighteous man: a man who did not know God at all, one who rejected Him, exclaimed Elihu. Job wondered, why should one try to live a life that pleases God? His stance and disposition: what was the point, if God was only going to unjustly judge one's righteousness and purity? This was Job's mindset, derived from his pain and affliction. Job felt he deserved more from the hand of God.

Elihu strongly expressed that God could not do evil; it was not associated with His character. God would always repay each person what they deserved, period. God would not say one thing and do another. Elihu asked who is above God and who directs Him to move or to reign? Who set God in charge? Who is His master? Who does God answer to? If God became nothing, this world and everything that dwells in it would become nothing as well, expressed Elihu.

The young man continued, God was everyone's reason for mere existence. Without the breath He breathed into man, what was his substance? Elihu endeavored to get those men to understand, God was just; He was above all! He posed a question to them, asking, were they going to cast down the One who was most honorable and upright? (Job 34:17). Then, the young man explained, it was God who judged kings and nobles, the poor and the rich. God saw all men the same; no one could hide from Him. All men of high and low status would see the grave, but not <u>God Almighty, the Righteous!</u>

In Job 34:26–30, Elihu said, God punished the wicked because they refused to honor Him. They oppressed the poor and the poor cried out to God and He answered. When God spoke a decree, who could challenge Him? If God took away His hand, who could seek it out? It was confirmed that God would give those who had done evil their just due, whether they offended one person or an entire nation. The hypocrites would not prevail. If they did, the people who had been afflicted would remain in bondage. That was not the way of God.

Then, Elihu rebuked the four men: Job, Eliphaz, Bildad, and Zophar. He expressed that none of them went before God to ask for *forgiveness. After all the wrong they had done, pointing fingers and offending God's character, they had not come to the realization that they had sinned. They didn't confess to God the wrongs they had done, nor make a promise to God that they would change their ways, eschewing (shunning) evil. If there was not any repentance or humility, how could God grant them forgiveness? That was a decision that they had to make for themselves, to humble themselves by their confessions and truly <u>repent</u> (turning away from their wrongdoings).*

Again, Elihu informed Job that his speech resembled that of a wicked man who did not know God. Elihu desired that Job would be dealt with accordingly by the hand of God, giving Job much-needed discipline to teach him the error of his ways.

Job was truly a wretch undone. He spoke foolishly before God about everything he was facing, and his friends did the same. There is such an awesome thing with Job's experience, though: with all of his harsh words, expressions of abandonment, and self-righteousness, *Job never cursed God.* God didn't view any part of how Job had dealt with his appointed time of affliction as a curse to Him. Look at the grace and mercy God allotted Job as he traveled through this period of unfamiliar torment, pain, and affliction. In his ignorance, God kept him! God knew the measure of grace He set out for Job's life.

"For by grace are ye saved through faith; and that not of yourselves: it is the gift of God: Not of works, lest any man should boast."
Ephesians 2:8-9

I have learned a vital point as it relates to our individual relationships with God: God requires brokenness. Brokenness is a sign of humility and submission. It shows God that we realize that we can't live without him because we are not perfect. It is okay that we are not perfect. It is okay that we are a mess! The best thing, and what God wants us to realize, is that we are not altogether whole. Only God is righteous! No matter how much we fast and pray and seek God . . . we, you, I will always need something from our Creator. We, you, I will always lack something. It's only by the grace of God and through faith we are made whole. It is through the sacrifice of Jesus Christ that we are able to be presented faultless, blameless, and holy before God. We ourselves can never do that—ever. We need the blood of Jesus. We needed God to send His Son, Jesus Christ, to be slain and crucified on the cross that He could rise again to save us, to complete us.

There is great strength in realizing we are not perfect. When we are searching for a fault within ourselves so that we might repent and ask God to help us, and we realize we can't find one: congratulations, the fault has been discovered. We were created with faults; this flesh is made up of sinfulness, wickedness, selfishness, immorality, etc. Simply put, it is full of bad stuff. So, we should always live broken and humble before God. God said, "ye shall be holy, for I am Holy" (Leviticus 11:45). We can certainly do this because He commanded it. God made provisions for us to carry out this command. We must realize though, there is nothing we can do within ourselves that can make us holy, no matter how much and how hard we try. (Side Bar: This doesn't give us an excuse not to try and not to do our very best.) Again, the only way we can become holy is by the application of grace, and through faith made available to us through the sacrifice of Jesus Christ.

Job was named perfect and upright, he avoided evil and was the greatest man in the east, yet he had this great lack. He offered sacrifices for himself and extra sacrifices for his children, and simply honored God with all of his house and substance, but Job was still very flawed. It's recorded that Job was rebuked by Elihu because he didn't humble himself and recognize that he wasn't above correction. Elihu explained to Job, in so many words, the only being that is righteous and perfect is God!

75

Though Job was known in the land to fear God, his speeches to his friends revealed that he had developed an "I can't do any wrong" complex. Yes, even God said that Job was perfect and upright, etc., and that was undoubtedly the life Job lived, but that didn't place him above his current circumstance and affliction. We must remember what Job failed to remember: we must remain humble before God. Even when we are deeply embedded in a situation that we feel is below us, we must "humble ourselves in the sight of the Lord . . ." (James 3:10). Because we are not flawless, we must realize there is something God is trying to work both out of us and in us. We are never above a buff! Honestly, we need all the buffing God chooses to allow because, truth be told, to reach God—not to be God, but to just reach God—takes an entire lifetime. Once we realize that we, within ourselves, will always need God—once we drop that defense and admit that, alone, we are imperfect and incomplete, God can work on us and use us for His glory.

Sovereign God Is He

Elihu, the young man, further poured wisdom into Job by questioning him, causing him to think. He asked, did he think it was wise to say that God was not more righteous than himself? Elihu was baffled at how it was possible for Job to say out of his mouth: what's the use of living a righteous life, and how does it benefit him? Elihu told him to look around at everything God created and take in the greatness of God. He pointed out: if we do wrong habitually or if we are living innocent lives, we still would not add to God or take away from His essence! We benefit from living righteously, not God. He was and would always be, with or without our willingness to serve Him. Living a hypocritical life would, again, only have a direct effect on man (Job 35:8). God, though, would reward each lifestyle. It was He who blessed and cursed, He who added and took away.

The oppressed (wicked) "cry out by reason of the arm of the mighty" (Job 35:9). Though they cried out because of their pain, they did not call out to God for their deliverance. They did not acknowledge or realize they needed Him beyond their current situation, so God ignored their worthless and empty pleas. He refused to answer and see to their needs because they only wanted relief from their pain and oppressor, without the necessary humility. If they had mustered up the gall to call out to God and asked for His help, He still wouldn't have turned His ear to them because they lacked sincere hearts. Since they were content in living the way they wanted and chose to, He turned a deaf ear toward them. Then Elihu explained, if God treated them that way, what did Job and his friends think He would do to those who were aware of His might and His mercy yet get frustrated with His timing (losing faith, trust, and patience in Him)? Because God was not moving according to their time and expectation, they had become restless and agitated with Him—what would He have to say to them?

Job believed that God did not hold to His word concerning the rewards of the wicked. He believed God to be absent. One thing Elihu needed Job to understand is that whether he witnessed God moving or not, He was the One who still held the power of judgment; He still sat on the throne. He was still God and for that he must trust Him always.

> **"Although thou sayest thou shalt not see Him, yet judgment is before Him; therefore trust thou in Him."**
> **Job 35:14**

Job's words were very rash and foolishly spoken against God. Through this time of suffering, Job found out he did not possess wisdom and understanding; he wasn't as innocent and righteous as he thought. Job got a serious wake up call to the reality of it all (Job 35:16).

Elihu continued, "Behold God is mighty, and despiseth [hate] not any: He is mighty in strength and wisdom" (Job 36:5). He begged their patience as he explained further the might and way of God. He also assured them, again, that he was not talking off the top of his head, but was speaking truly from the heart of God.

The young man explained that God did not spare those who were wicked in their hearts, but He had great mercy on those who were poor. God kept close watch on the pure in heart and set them up as kings; God exalted them forever. He had a special protection over the righteous.

Elihu said if the righteous then find themselves restrained and entangled in the sins of this world, God would show them their mistakes. God opened their understanding to their sins and instructed them to repent. If they turned from their wicked ways and heeded His commands, He would bless them. Through His forgiveness and their obedience, He would cause them to be consumed in His goodness and mercy. If His children refused to obey and turn from their ways, He would cause them to suffer and die. The grave would receive them because their ignorance and disobedience drove them there.

"For truly my words shall not be false: he that is perfect in knowledge is with thee."
Job 36:4

Furthermore, Elihu explained, the hypocrites, who were evil to the core, allowed anger to accumulate. The wicked, being so full of evil, didn't even shed a tear and express any remorse at God's correction (Job 36:13).

They rested in such evil. Even when God caused distress to come upon them, they did not desire to change their ways; repentance was far from them. They were surrounded by the like-minded, and their days were very short on the earth. On the other hand, God heard the cries of those who were afflicted yet endeavoring to live an honorable and righteous life. God delivered them.

Additionally, Elihu expressed that God would have taken Job out of his misery and would have provided him with plenty to satisfy him, but Job had spoken without wisdom, like the wicked. Job was

78

instructed to be careful of what he did and what he said because God could easily hold back His forgiveness and take his life.

Elihu expressed to Job: there was no type of ransom or exchange that could save him. He then asked, would God receive riches in lieu of his suffering? Would Job's riches make up for his sins? Would God regard Job's strength above His own and restore him?

Do Not Desire Darkness

Job desired darkness to consume him, but Elihu encouraged him to reject the desire to dwell in a place where lives were destroyed. Elihu surely spoke with much wisdom and from the heart of God. He admonished Job to stop esteeming wickedness over affliction and distress. While Job defended his innocence, sin had unconsciously become his choice (Job 36:21). The Word says in Psalms 66:18, "If I regard [esteem] sin in my heart, the Lord will not hear me." This Scripture magnifies the exact statements Elihu spoke to Job.

Elihu so passionately articulated the greatness of God and how matchless He was! Who could instruct God—who was wiser than He? (Job 36:22). No one was on the same level as God or could teach as He did. No one else possessed His wisdom and infinite knowledge. Who could give God understanding? No one could give a statement concerning God's character vouching for any evil He had done (Job 36:22–23).

Moreover, Elihu explained, we cannot forget that God was who caused us to bring Him glory. It is through our existence that others witness His great work, and we praise Him for it. He said, our understanding is very limited of the greatness of the Creator: ancient of days. Before us, before the great number of days of this world, God was, and after us He would still be. The young man expressed: God created and formed the rain drops which come from the waters stored up in the clouds over the whole world. Who could fathom this great system, and the mystery of the loud thunder which came from the place God dwelled? God orchestrated the lightning and reached the immeasurable depth of the seas. This was the same great God who provided enough food to feed the entire world, and who directed and commanded the thunder and lightning to land in a specific place. All of creation understood that after the thunder made its roar, a storm followed. We may not be able to comprehend the wisdom behind it all, but God has blessed us to acknowledge the signs of His great work (Job 36:25–33).

God Is in Control

In Elihu's conclusion, he spoke of the unsearchable wisdom and understanding of the might of God. He mentioned, again, how the thunder's great sound startled and frightened him. He encouraged Job to take note of the strength of God's voice. Once again, God controlled and directed the lightning to flash under the heavens,

"God thundereth marvelously with His voice; great things doeth He, which we cannot comprehend."
Job 37:5

throughout the earth. As Elihu expressed, thunder was understood to be the voice of God; its strength He did not restrain.

Furthermore, Elihu said, we would never fully understand God's ways because His wisdom was concealed within Himself. God commanded snow to fall on the earth, and rain drops to pour down upon it, in abundance or sparingly. He controlled it all, and no one would be able to stand up and take His glory.

God allowed the earth to be covered in abundance with either snow or rain, causing all men to cease work, even causing the animals to cease and be confined to their homes. No one and not one thing would get God's glory.

God sent storms from the south and cold temperatures by many winds from the north, exclaimed Elihu. By the breath of God, ice was formed, causing the broad seas to be consumed by it (Job 37:10). At that time, in the winter months, God would spread both full clouds of water and concealed lightning throughout the skies to make the skies clear. When God spoke to the clouds, they obeyed His voice (Job 37:12). The different kinds of weather that were experienced all over the world—winds, storms, ice, snow, rain, thunder, and lightning—were all used either for chastisement, to simply nurture the land, or to show compassion, as expressed in Job 37:13. These weather conditions were signs, and they were all designed with a meaning and a purpose; God created them to be such.

> *"He sealeth up the hand of every man; that all men may know His work."*
> *Job 37:7*

Elihu insisted that Job listen closely as he explained God's might and wondrous acts. He needed Job to understand clearly and to differentiate who he was and who God was. Elihu asked Job if he understood the mysteries behind just one aspect of God's creation: the clouds. Did he understand the instructions that only the clouds were specifically designed to understand? Had God secretly spoken to him about the mysteries behind the seasons: how one day there was extreme heat of summer, and the next day bitter cold of winter? Had he helped God extend the skies over the entire world? (Job 37:18).

Elihu needed Job to understand that we would never ever understand such great wisdom and knowledge. We would remain in complete darkness compared to our great King. God had to teach us these great things—we could not stumble upon this wisdom ourselves. If we tried to stand before God and speak of such things, trying to command and instruct Him, we would be brought to great shame (Job 37:20).

Equally important, after all the clouds were spread throughout the skies, was that no man could look up into the sun and behold it. Even though it rested countless miles away, it still shone too bright for our eyes to gaze into. For that matter, it was certain that we could not see into the eyes and glory of our great God that we may know His ways and His reasons. He was more glorious than the sun, which He created, formed, and was the source of. We could never behold His majesty, which was far beyond the sun!

> *"Touching the Almighty, we cannot find Him out: He is excellent in power, and in judgment and in plenty of justice: He will not afflict."*
> *Job 37:23*

God is great and pure. He will not cause us harm unjustly! He will not cause us to suffer for no apparent cause; He will hold to His Word and reward us with His judgment. <u>God holds great mercy and grace, and unconditional and incomparable love that consumes us beyond our comprehension!</u> He does not will or desire for us to be destroyed. God holds fast to His Word and His promises; He is not sluggish or negligent concerning them. The Word says, in 2 Peter 3:9, "The Lord is not slack concerning His promise, as some men count slackness; but is longsuffering to us-ward, not willing that any should perish, but that all should come to repentance."

While men reverence and honor who God is, God refuses to have respect and honor for those who are wise in their own heart. If you believe you are righteous by your own hand, God will not preserve or turn towards you.

In Proverbs 14:12 it says, "There is a way that seemeth right unto a man, but the end thereof are the ways of death." If you don't submit to God and bow to His majesty, He won't have any regard toward you. A nugget to take away from this: don't be wise in your own heart, believing that your way is *the* way. God is greater. He is in total control, always and forever.

I've learned when we are defensive, as Job was, and as I often am, we are fighting God's mighty hand. God wants to give us better and give us more, *but* we fight Him daily in the process. The Scripture

Psalms 51:17 says that "a broken and contrite heart, O God, thou wilt[will] not despise [hate]." God will not turn away from you if you have a contrite heart, because that is the heart He acknowledges and deeply desires. We must become low—very low—to experience the greatness of our great King! In the book of Job, he, along with his friends, Elihu, and even God, spoke and said: who can contend against God? If we are fighting God tooth and nail, if we are kicking and screaming against the hand and the will of God, who do we think will win? We must submit our entire being to God and realize only He is righteous! Only God is righteous!

"Men do therefore fear him: He respecteth not any that are wise of heart."
Job 37:24

I would strongly suggest that we read, recite, and set Psalms 51:1–17 deep within our spirit, because this is the heart that God hears. He hears a heart that is humble, fragmented, sorrowful, and repentant—yet grateful and thankful. God hears a heart that realizes it is incomplete and evil by nature, a nature that cannot enter or inherit the Kingdom of God or the unrestrained blessings of God.

Remember, God requires brokenness. We will always be lower than God, but connected to Him through our faith in Jesus Christ. Thank You, Lord! Jesus Christ completes us and presents us holy, faultless, and blameless before God. Without Christ and our faith in Him, without the blood He shed for us, we are forever incomplete. If we ever approach God without being broken and humbled, He won't hear us. Again, Psalms 66:18 says, "If I [we] regard iniquity in my [our] heart, the Lord will not hear me [us]." God requires nothing less than brokenness and humility, because of His unmatched perfection and completeness, and His desire to make us whole.

CHAPTER 8

The Lord Speaks:
Journey to Restoration
(Job 38-42)

God and Job

After being silent from the beginning of Job's affliction, God broke His silence. His questioning of Job was extensive, allowing Job to once again recognize his rightful place.

God said to Job: was he there when the worlds were formed? More specifically, was Job there to give morning its designated place? Was Job worthy or big enough to challenge the law of God? God put pressure on Job, a mere man, and insisted that he answered the questions He had (Job 38:3). God asked Job, where was he when the foundations of the world were laid? He made certain Job knew he was not worthy to contend with Him. God made Job think deeply about everything he had said towards Him and about Him to his friends. After Elihu spoke and put Job in his place, God came to confirm every word.

Did Job Think He Was Equal with God?

God asked Job: who controlled the waves of the sea? And had he been in the depths of death, where his eyes had beheld the gates of Hell? Was Job aware of how broad the earth was spread? God said to Job, "declare if thou knowest it all?" (Job 38:18). God urged Job to speak up if He was wrong, or if he could relate to such great wisdom. If Job knew as much as God did, God wanted to know. Now, God knew very well what Job knew and that he could not possibly compare to Himself, but God needed Job to understand that. If Job understood the wisdom that only God contained, He didn't want Job to remain silent.

Job had challenged God in his pain and suffering, saying things that were very foolish concerning God. He truly lacked wisdom and understanding in this place: God knew. Therefore, God prepared Job's necessary measure from the very thought of Job, before conception.

God reproved Job through many questions. He asked Job about the mysteries behind creation: where was light when darkness was present, and vice versa? If Job knew the answer, did he know because he spoke it into existence, or because he was there when it was spoken into existence? God wanted Job to think about how old he was and how much older light, darkness, and creation was (Job 38:21). Did Job really have the number of days recorded and committed to memory? Were not his days limited? What was the wisdom behind the snow and hail? When clouds were scattered, where did they dwell? God enlightened Job that where no man dwelled, rain still fell there. He still took care of that land because He created it, but Job could not have possibly known it. The land may be deserted and all alone, but God still caused grass to grow there. Life was still there (Job 38:27).

Perhaps Job had control over the rain and told it when to fall and where. God asked, what was dew and where did it come from? Who created and formed the ice; how was it possible for an entire ocean to freeze? Who controlled the stars and determined the seasons of the zodiac and guided the "Bear Guard"? Was it possible for Job to know the insides and outskirts of the heavens and control what went on in the earth, simultaneously? Did creation yield to Job's voice? Did it know him? Who provided food for the lions and their cubs, which lived in the wild; who made sure the birds of the air found food to satisfy them and their babies?

Furthermore, God asked, who was there when the goats, which too lived in the wild, bore their kids? Could Job know? Did he provide food for them that they may grow in strength and learn to fend for themselves? Who took care of the donkeys, who gained strength from the grass? Perhaps the ox, strong as it is, would listen to Job and obey his every word? Maybe Job understood the very makeup of the peacock, whose feathers were beautiful and uniquely designed? Or did he understand the ostrich, which left her eggs buried in the ground, failing to remember where she hid them (Job 39:14–15)? God had blinded this creature so that she had no regard for what may happen to her babies. God did not create her with that wisdom or concern. God took care of the eggs. He designed it that specific way for His specific reason. The ostrich was made to fly above the horses, looking down as it mocked the horses for their limited ability. Job simply did not know. God was enlightening him: it was He who fashioned such a creature!

Then God spoke about the beauty of the horses. He asked Job if their strength came from his own hand. Was Job the crafty hand behind the horses' beautiful details, from their manes, to their wide nostrils, to their shoes? Was Job who fashioned them to jump as effortlessly as a grasshopper? God was the One who created horses strong and fearless, and to face wars and battles head on.

Furthermore, was it at the command of Job that the hawks flew about the earth? Was it at his command that the eagle soared way above the clouds, flying higher than any other fowl? Eagles were designed to experience the world from very high up; their view was very special. God was who provided for their young and made them to feed off the dead that they may be satisfied.

> **"Doth the hawk fly by thy wisdom, and stretch her wings toward the south?"**
> **Job 39:26**

God asked Job, was he worthy enough to question Him and find fault with Him? God had encouraged Job, once again, to bring whatever problem he had with Him to His attention. God desired Job to show Him where He made a wrong turn and where He lacked. Whoever could chastise and correct God, He desired for him to do so (Job 40:2).

While God brought so many questions to Job, we can very well replace Job's name with our own. So many times, we experience painful and frustrating situations in our lives and become mad at God, as if He did something wrong. Then we feel the need to confront or question Him on what He is doing. Did God make a wrong decision concerning us and the things He has allowed to come our way? Cannot He do as He pleases with us and all His creation? Did He not create the earth and ". . . the fullness thereof; the world and they that dwell therein"? (Psalms 24:1). Did He not place us, His creation—you and I—in it to dwell? Again, I'll mention that we are not above suffering and being corrected. Our hard times are given to us that we may be corrected and become better. The suffering is for our own good, not God's. God is already correct and whole.

Job had so much to say during his suffering, neglecting to realize He was challenging God. As I have mentioned before, we can very well express our hearts and concerns to God—He wants us to—but we must remember who He is and who we are: Creator and creation. He can do whatever He wants to do; what He does is for our betterment and perfection, and for His glory. He is the potter and we are the big lump of clay. He is the goldsmith and we are the piece of gold beneath a worthless exterior, before being placed in the fire. Our suffering is to uncover the greatness that He embedded in us from the foundations of the world. In our "Journey to Restoration," we must acknowledge and remember who God is and know without a shadow of doubt that God has our best interest at heart: He loves us.

Job's Eyes Became Open

Job was finally able to speak, but he did not say much. Job was even more distraught than before, but in this moment, he was brought very low—humbled. Job said, "Behold, I am vile [foul]; what shall I answer thee? I will lay mine hand upon my mouth. Once have I spoken; but I will not answer: yea, twice; but I will proceed no further" (Job 40:4–5). Job finally admitted he was wicked and unworthy, that he had stumbled and was wrong. Because his knowledge was certainly finite compared to God and all of His wisdom and righteousness, he was now able to understand that he had absolutely no place to question God the way he did. Job had spoken foolishly before, but he refused to make that mistake again. He chose to no longer speak because he realized he was not who and what he had once claimed to be. At this point, Job was acknowledging that he spoke without knowledge and wisdom, as Elihu had pointed out to him.

God was speaking to Job out of a storm. He was angry with Job and making him aware that he was a mere man created by His mighty and perfect hands. For the second time, God was putting Job in his place. He was illustrating to Job the distinct difference between where he stood and where He would always stand. By the completion of this necessary chastisement and reproof, Job would be very clear. His friends, who were still close by, would be clear as well.

God proceeded to ask Job questions as they related to the wisdom of creation. He asked: was he wise or mighty enough to question God's judgment and find flaws? Was Job righteous, and had now found in that righteousness the courage to cast down God? Was Job as powerful and as strong as God? Could his voice be heard over the earth as the mighty sound of thunder?

"Gird up thy loins now like a man."
Job 40:7

Since Job had questioned God so much and recognized himself as faultless, God presented Job the opportunity to prove himself. "Make yourself beautiful, since you have that great ability!" This was God's disposition. If Job could bury all the wicked together, then God would have honored and praised him. God would have given Job the respect he deserved if he could have proven himself in that manner—showing God that he had the power and strength to save himself (Job 40:14).

God Contends Effortlessly Against Creation

God then brought to Job's attention a behemoth, which is said to be a hippopotamus. God expressed: He created this beast as he did man. It, just as an ox, fed on grass. It was strong and its power came from the core of its belly. God described the extent of its strength: it was as strong as a tree, and "His bones are as strong as pieces of brass; his bones are like bars of iron."(Job 40:18). The behemoth's thighs were strengthened by closely knitted tendons.

According to the scriptures, the behemoth was known to be the first animal with such power and strength by the might of God, but He made this strong and powerful creature obey the strength of His mere words. This creature could be well hidden as it rested under the trees, covered by the reeds. For that reason, no one could seek out and destroy it.

The behemoth was great in strength and not intimidated by the waters. Because it was so heavy and solid, the waters could not overtake it. Its eyes were always open, so it was very alert. Its nose was strong enough to protect itself against any trap. God, through this animal, was illustrating to Job His great strength; God was greater than this great beast. <u>Though its bones were strong as brass and iron, God could effortlessly contend against it. God created the behemoth (hippopotamus), and with all its might and power it was still no match for the incomparable power and strength of a single word spoken out of the mouth of God.</u>

Then God brought another great animal, the leviathan, known as a sea monster or crocodile (both great in strength), to Job's attention. God was boasting about another beast of the water, illustrating how fearless and great it was. God posed a few questions to Job, yet again, about this beast. Was it possible for Job to catch it with a fish hook or a rope? Would this animal ask anything of Job, as if he were capable of supplying it? God made Job think: was he confident enough to entertain or approach the sea monster/crocodile the same way he would present himself before a bird? Could Job get a spear through the leviathan's thick skin and capture it? God assured Job: if he went to touch this beast, or attempted to catch it, he would never do it again because he would be destroyed! (Job 41:8).

God expressed distinctly: every man was extremely afraid of this beast because it was so vicious. The mere sight of it terrified people. The thought of taking complete control over it was simply foolish. The leviathan was much too strong and dangerous for a man to interact with. There was no creature quite like it. If no one could stand before this great sea monster that crept upon the earth, then, who would be able to challenge God in all His strength, might, and wisdom?

God took great pride in bringing this beast that He had created, before Job. It profoundly illustrated God's glory! No one could approach it with a bridle, nor could someone ride on its thick skin, so uniquely designed. No one could challenge the leviathan! Its teeth and its bite were to be feared (Job 41:14). It was a lethal tool, used to devour the

"He [leviathan] esteemeth iron as straw, and brass as rotten wood."
Job 41:27

biggest and strongest of animals. Its skin being tightly joined was the beauty of it. The leviathan was a unique creature, as smoke came from its nostrils and its breath was as hot as lit coals (Job 41:18–19). Its neck was where its strength rested. Though the leviathan caused great distress to its prey, it took pure joy in being fed. Its chest was as hard as stones, and when it rose to defend itself, many of the toughest men were frightened. The leviathan was so strong that swords and guns could not pierce it.

Nothing was a great challenge for this sea monster. Its strength and might caused it to stand against darts, arrows, and sling stones. Those weapons were not strong or threatening enough to make it flinch. As it moved about the bottom of the waters, it left a trail behind. It troubled the waters and uprooted anything planted. The leviathan, also, disrupted any other sea creature in its path; it was ruthless and fearless. All the sea creatures, as well as any animals by the wayside, feared it. The trail that was left behind the leviathan glistened, making its presence known for sure (Job 41:32).

"He maketh the deep to boil like a pot: he maketh the sea like a pot of ointment."
Job 41:31

God explained to Job there was not any other animal with such might and strength, and which was as fearless. This beast was a king and, again, took on the strongest of the animals. He asked Job, since he had so much to say, could he stand up against this animal and contend with it? God expressed to Job that by His hands were created both he and the great leviathan.

Job's Humility Re-Established

After God finished speaking, Job admitted his error before God and his friends. He saw even clearer and understood that he was not faultless. Job acknowledged that God sat above the whole world and upon the heavens, and nothing was hidden from His sight. God could freely do whatever He wanted, and there was not a thing anyone could do to restrain Him: He is God.

Job was very grieved! He confessed to speaking without understanding and wisdom towards God. He took full responsibility for wrongfully questioning God's wisdom and His righteousness. Job realized that these things were too great and mysterious for him to know and he was extremely sorrowful. He was now reproved, plainly seeing his ignorance.

God showed Job His might and strength through His creations. As Job had patterned his life after what he was taught by his elders, he had obtained a close bond with God. But God desired more for their relationship—one where He could share a greater depth of who He was with him. Job was obedient to those customs and feared God the only way he knew how: through his sacrifices and honorable lifestyle. He was perfect, and in a class of his own in the earth—God vouched for that (Job 1:1). But, again, Job lacked a more

"I have heard of thee by the hearing of the ear: but now mine eye seeth Thee."
Job 42:5

personal relationship with God, which God wanted with him. Through Satan tampering with Job's life, Job was now made to see and experience God on a totally different level. Job now saw, for himself, who God was because God had allowed him to suffer such affliction and chastisement.

Job was perfect, as God proclaimed, but still flawed. One thing was sure: at the very core of Job, he loved God. Everything he experienced and learned prior to these tests proved that God had a special place in Job's heart. Also, God loved Job so much that He covered him in all of his ignorance. After Job expressed how much he despised himself, he immediately asked God for forgiveness!

"Wherefore I abhor [hate] myself, and repent in dust and ashes."
Job 42:6

Job's eyes were opened!

God's Instructions to Restoration

Finally, God spoke directly to Eliphaz, expressing how angry He was with him and his two friends, Bildad and Zophar. God was angry with them because they spoke foolishly, as Job had done (Job 42:7). God instructed them to offer up burnt offerings of bullocks (oxen) and rams. They were commanded to take it all to Job and have <u>Job</u> pray for them. God would only hear Job's prayer. Only then, would God have mercy on them and not deal with them according to their foolishness. They all did what God told them, and God accepted their offerings and the prayer sent up for them by Job.

In all of Job's anger and disappointment towards his friends, and the sense of betrayal by them, Job had to truly act in humility and pray for his friends, who weren't showing themselves as friendly. This was also a humbling experience for Job's three friends because the very one they thought was a hypocrite—wicked and unworthy to stand before God—had to act on their behalf. For their sins to be forgiven, they had to ask Job to pray for them. After Job's obedience to God—praying for the very ones who beat him down and caused more grief than comfort in the most treacherous time of his life—God restored all that Job lost.

God caused all of Job's family to come back into his life, as well as all of those who knew him before his time of affliction. They all came to Job's house to eat and celebrate with him. They loved on him and "comforted him over all the evil that the Lord had brought upon him" (Job 42:11). He was showered with many gifts, money, and a gold earring from everyone in attendance. God gave Job double the number of sheep, camels, oxen, and she asses that he had before (Job 42:12). Job bore more children: seven sons and three daughters, as he had before. His daughters were more beautiful: "And in all the land were no women found so fair" (Job 42:15). Job gave his children their inheritance, and he lived an additional 140 years, witnessing four generations. After much suffering, Job was favored to enjoy the abundant blessings of God: "So Job died, being old and full of days" (Job 42:17).

CHAPTER 9

God Knows Your Measure

Through Job's story, we have learned: Job blamed God, expressed how much he hated his life, and cursed the day he was born. Job said God made him His enemy, and had forsaken him. He and his friends pointed their fingers unjustly to one another, trying to prove how guilty and evil each one was. Job expressed, repeatedly, how unworthy he was of such suffering, pain, and affliction. All these things Job had done and said, yet he didn't curse God. I gave my thoughts earlier, but the question stands: what, then, is cursing God?

God knew Job was hurting, but God also knew it was time to take their relationship to another level. He offered up Job, at this appointed time, to rid Job of his impurities and simply draw Job closer to Him. Those impurities were hidden and covered, maybe even suppressed, by the laws he followed and the overall honorable and perfect lifestyle he lived. Even though he ". . . was perfect and upright [honest], and one that feared God, and eschewed [avoided] evil" (Job 1:1), he still had some issues that may have developed even while God blessed him so greatly and consistently. We don't always know what's in our character or what's in the core of us that isn't quite like God, until He allows us to suffer some things.

Following every word spoken by God, and having everything protected by the hand of God, can make us ignore our anger, pride, or lust for many different things. Over time, as we are blessed, we can get desensitized and fail to seek God as much as we should— because we have become comfortable. Our mindset could then be, "God must be pleased with me, so I'll keep doing the same thing I've been doing: being morally good, not intentionally sinning, going to church, being active in our ministries and communities, etc." When we become complacent, we stop asking God to purify us. We began to think unconsciously that we are already "pure"—we are okay, and in good standing with God.

Deception is thinking we are above being cleaned out. If we were pure and without fault, we would be sitting on God's throne. We simply are not. Trials must come to make us more like our Creator. Sufferings come to drive out the works of the flesh *(Galatians 5:19–21)*, and work in the fruit of the Spirit *(Galatians 5:22–23)*. That's when we will resemble pure gold—after the suppression of the flesh from the inside out.

Cursing God means blasphemous behaviors and thoughts that stem from our heart. If Job had stopped honoring God as God, because of the suffering he had to endure, he would have cursed God; or would have that been the case? No matter what Job felt, he stood on his hope in God, which was at the core of him. It is truly at the core of all of us, and it keeps us holding on beyond the foolishness we may say out of our pain and frustrations: *i.e., not from our heart.* I believe Job stood on the greatness and faithfulness of God.

Job believed in the relationship he built with God—the God he feared and the God he honored. Job knew of the great power, wisdom, and infinite knowledge of God. Job recognized, even when facing turmoil, God was still sitting on the throne. Yes, his flesh cried out and his words were harsh at times, but these are the things God was purging out of Job. Job held onto the authenticity of God, and everything he had grown to know God to be. Even through this pain, he knew God had a reason. Even if God never revealed that reason, Job knew it didn't diminish how great and incomparable God was. Job spoke foolishly, not realizing what he was saying. But as Elihu said to Job, Job was trying to defend and justify himself rather than focus on the beauty, innocence, and righteousness of God. Job just didn't understand, but God covered him with the necessary measure of grace he needed to pull through.

Had Job not lived a life worthy to be tried and proven of God prior to his affliction, God wouldn't have offered him up to Satan. God knew Job and had great confidence in him, but it wasn't because Job had some great ability within his members to not curse

100

God. God had great confidence in His love for Job because of Job's obedience and reverence for Him. <u>God's word went out concerning Job; therefore, in His own word was His surety.</u>

When God's word is spoken, it cannot come back to Him void. Isaiah 55:11 says, "So shall my word that goeth forth out of my mouth: it shall not return unto me void, but it shall accomplish that which I please and it shall prosper in the thing whereto I sent it." If God said it, we must know that it is! With God offering Job at the mercy of Satan, we recognize and understand that Job loved God and God was pleased with Him, but it was time for Job to come into a deeper covenant with Him. God absolutely knows the measure of grace, mercy, patience, hope, and faith we all need for us to line up with His Word. If God spoke a thing concerning us, it *is*! We should know: no matter what, if we are in His hands and delighting in Him, everything He causes and allows to come our way we will accomplish with great victory!

God knew that Job wasn't without fault, and wasn't as beautiful and innocent as Himself. God knew these things: He is God! God knew there were some kinks that needed to be straightened out in the very make up of Job. For these reasons, his suffering came. In all we have read and experienced in Job's story, we can agree that most of Job's responses seemed as if he cursed God, by our own standards. This shows that God is truly not like man.

God is aware of how much each individual needs of grace, forgiveness, mercy, patience, etc. If we trust God, we'll know that if He has allowed us to experience such grief, despair, pain, and affliction, He will also give us everything we need to survive it. The biggest thing to remember is we must trust God. The scripture says, "Trust in the Lord with all thine heart; and lean not to thine own understanding. In all thy ways acknowledge Him, and He shall direct thy paths" *(Proverbs 3:5–6).*

In this story, Job was in complete darkness as to what was going on. God had this conversation with Satan, not with anybody else. Job had no idea his life was about to be shaken in such a way. God had confidence in Job only because God had confidence in His own Word.

We can count on God to make the things He speaks of good: if God said it, He will do it! He knows what we need to help us walk and live in the likeness and image He created us in. We must trust the process, knowing that God is with us always. He will give us the needed tools and strength necessary to survive the specific assignments attached to our lives. Trust God!

"God is not a man that He shall lie; neither a Son of Man, that He shall repent: hath He said and shall He not do it? Or hath He spoken, and shall He not make it good?"
Numbers 23:19

Furthermore, because God said it, He gives the measure of grace and faith needed to fulfill His Word! Because of this, we are truly unable to judge one another. Not only are people unworthy to know and understand this measure enough to judge each other, we are unable and unworthy to judge ourselves. Job unjustly judged himself. We aren't made to know the depths of everything God will allow. He knows how evil and wicked this flesh is. What is over the top and unforgivable for us is not for our God. Thank You, Jesus! We mess up thinking we are in a position we are not, just as Job did. We should stay humble, and it is through our sufferings that we can.

We must realize God is our only judge. What is okay for one may not be okay for another. What is acceptable or excusable for me may not be for you, in God's eyes, based on our individual level of understanding.

Only God knows your measure!

Another great take away from this story: when we don't fully understand what a person is experiencing, it's vital to not speak too much on the situation. As we experienced in this story, Job's friends caused him more grief than comfort. They carried him to the edge of the cliff, simultaneously ripping off his parachute. Their words may have been from an honest and concerned place, yet it was killing Job. Job was loaded with a ton on his shoulders. Each of his friends, with their words, added another ton.

"For I say, through the grace given unto me, to every man that is among you, not to think of himself more highly than he ought to think; but to think soberly, according as God hath dealt to every man the measure of faith."
Romans 12:3

We must be careful we aren't driving our neighbor to curse God. Their situation may already seem impossible—then we come behind and push them closer and closer to the edge. We should be prayerful and ask God, before we do anything, how we should or could help our neighbor, our friend. We have to avoid looking on a circumstance and jumping in: we must pray.

Let us strive to grow, individually, in our relationship with God. Let us lean effortlessly on Him for everything. The scriptures say if we "draw nigh to God, He will draw nigh to [us]" (James 4:8). If we call out to God, He will hear us. If we ask, we will receive. If we only knock, the door(s) will be opened. If we seek, we will find! (Luke 11:9–10). And if we search for God with all our hearts, it is definite that He will see to our needs (Jeremiah 29:13).

"And ye shall seek, me, and find me, when ye shall search for me with all your heart."
Jeremiah 29:13

If we purpose in our hearts to be closer to God daily, when our friends or neighbors need godly counsel, we will be a helpful avenue. This is simply because we have learned to continually seek God for His wisdom and direction. Let us care for one another as we care for ourselves. We don't want just anybody speaking off the top of their head in lieu of helping us. We will always desire sound advice or company to aid us in our ultimate deliverance. As I mentioned earlier, sometimes that wisdom will direct us to just sit quietly with our friend, as Job's friends did the first few days they arrived at his house. And we will have to follow God's lead and do just that.

Let us strive for wisdom, which can only be found in the heart of God. A scripture will not always help our friend and neighbor in a place of unfamiliarity and affliction, especially if we smother them with it. The popular statement "You will make it through this: God will turn it around," in lieu of encouragement, will not always help to heal the open wound, mend the broken heart, or release the battered soul. It will not always regulate a troubled mind. Let us intentionally seek God, the giver of wisdom, for greater wisdom—wisdom beyond where we have grown, in order to be a sound and solid help.

Prayer

As we come to the close of this book, please join with me in prayer:

Father in the name of Jesus,
We come to you in prayer thanking You for all things. Thank you for the breath You breathe into us! Thank you for keeping us and giving us the endurance we need to make it. Thank You for strengthening us to bear our most trying experiences! Thank you for speaking Your reliable and immovable word over our lives that we may live. Above all, thank You for being God, the matchless King!

God, we understand now, You know our very measure. From creation, You poured that measure into us that we may abide under the shadow and safety of Your wings. Almighty God, our Father and King, we adore You and give You all the honor, glory, and praise! God, we ask that You continue to show us how much You care. We are empty vessels desiring daily to be used by You. Fill us up that we may please You, and strengthen us with Your might. God, help us to realize You will never let us go.

We are learning, day after day, how to trust You more. It comforts us to know, even though we may seem to be failing, You know our measure! You know how much we can handle. Just when we feel like we cannot take life anymore, You will always send Your help to save us! So, Lord, help us to enable You to be that help. God, Our peace rests in Your truth and infinite ability.

Lord, wherever we find ourselves, let us always remember You gave us all we need to survive. We thank You for loving us and choosing us to glorify you! We love you from the depths of our heart and soul!

In Jesus' name
Amen

About the Author

Crystal (Tate) Roberts, 33, was born and raised in Prince George's County, Maryland, to her amazing parents: the late Patricia Ann (Lloyd) Tate-Graham, and Robert Walter Tate, Sr. Crystal is the ninth child of the "Tate Eleven" born of their union. She believes the greatest gift her parents could have given was introducing her and her siblings to the Lord in their youth.

Being raised in the church, Crystal's love and desire for God captured her before she could fully comprehend it. She has been committed to God ever since. While serving 16 years at Bethel Deliverance Outreach Ministries, Inc. in Upper Marlboro, Maryland, under the leadership of Pastor Alonzo M. Walker, Sr. and First Lady Wanda Walker, she gained a strong foundation of faith, dedication to God and ministry, along with a personal relationship with God.

After receiving a prophetic word from Apostle Dr. Keith K. Curry, she later transitioned to Jacksonville, North Carolina where she is now a dedicated member of Free and Independent Apostolic Church, Inc. Shortly after her faith-move, she met and married her loving and hardworking husband, Roderick. Crystal enjoys: serving in the church, singing, dancing, songwriting, journaling, cooking, baking, and spending time at the park, when she isn't working in the salon. She loves nature and spending time with her family, both spiritual and natural.

Through everything Crystal has experienced in her life, she has gripped her faith in God and His ability to guide and carry her and pull her through. Through the good and the bad, she has learned to hold fast to the Word of God. In her journey as a believer, two of her favorite scriptures that give her endurance are Jeremiah 29:11, "For I know the thoughts I think towards you, saith the Lord, thoughts of peace, and not of evil, to give you an expected end"; and Proverbs

3:5-6, "Trust in the Lord with all thine heart, and lean not to thine own understanding. In all thy ways acknowledge Him, and He shall direct thy paths."

Her encouragement to her readers is, "Brethren, be strong in the Lord and in the power of His might" (Ephesians 6:10). You can make it through everything that God has allowed and will allow to come your way. Put all your trust in God.

"God bless His people everywhere."
-Patricia Tate-Graham

Made in the USA
Columbia, SC
16 March 2021